Adventures in New Lands: Volume 9

Other titles in this series

Volume 1: *Inuit Folk-tales* by Knud Rasmussen
Volume 2: *Journal in Greenland* by Hans Egede
Volume 3: *Vikings of Today* by Wilfred Grenfell
Volume 4: *Tales of Yukaghir* by Waldemar Bogoras
Volume 5: *Eden of the North* by Signe Rink
Volume 6: *Diary of Johannes Hansen*
Volume 7: *Singnagtigaq* by Mathias Storch
Volume 8: *Inuit Poems and Songs*
collected by William Thalbitzer
Voulme 9: *Tuumarsi* by Frederik Nielsen
Volume 10: *Kayakmen* collected by Signe Rink

This book is translated and published in agreement with Det Grønlandske Selskab (The Greenlandic Society) in Denmark, which first published it in Danish in 1980. Tuumarsi is translated from Greenlandic by the author after the original version, Tûmarse kinguâríngnik okalugtuak, 1934.

Funded in part by
DANISH ARTS FOUNDATION
Copenhagen, Denmark

First English edition

Design: IPI Press

ISBN 978-0-9961938-3-2

✦

International Polar Institute Press
Post Office Box 212
Hanover, New Hampshire 03755 USA

Tuumarsi

By Frederik Nielsen

Translated by Torben Hutchings

IPI

Distributed by University Press of New England
upne.com

Contents

Introduction

by Christian Berthelsen

We know the original and traditional Greenlandic form of storytelling from the oral traditions, namely the legends, which have luckily been preserved for posterity through their collection and printing in Greenlandic and Danish.

The growing influence from Western Europe in cultural matters resulted in, among other things, a new form of prose and poetry. In 1914 the first Greenlandic novel, in the modern sense, was published. This was Mathias Storch's "Sinnattugaq" *(IPI Press English editon published 2016).* 17 years later, in 1931, Augo Lynge published "*Ukiut 300-nngornerat*" ("The 300th year after Hans Egede's arrival"), and Frederik Nielsen's "*Tuumarsi*" (Thomas), which published in 1934, became the third on the list. The two former novels are, in reality, political writings, and both address the future of Greenland. Contrary to these, the plot of the novel "*Tuumarsi*" goes back in time, as the idea has been obtained from an authentic event in the middle of the 19th century, when the inhabitants of a little settlement somewhere in western Greenland caved in to hunger during a period of poor hunting.

"*Tuumarsi*" is a tremendously realistic depiction of the people in a little village community—of the light side of life, as well as its darkness. The life depicted is far from idyllic. The eternal struggle to exist forms the common denominator of the entire storyline. The psyche and humor is particularly Greenlandic, as Frederik Nielsen knew them during his childhood in a settlement among them. It is a truthful depiction and an ethnographically correct picture of the life of the hunter.

A bit of practical information: All the names in the book are European or biblical, even if they might look Greenlandic to Danish readers, for they are written as they are said and pronounced in Greenlandic. *Tuumarsi* (*t* pronounced as *d*) is, as mentioned, Thomas, while his wife is called *Kaluliit* (Karoline), and their sons Timuuto (Themotius—the first *t* pronounced like a Danish "t" and the last as a *d*) and Iisaaq (Isak)—simply to mention a few examples.

The book's author, Frederik Nielsen, was a promising young man at the time he wrote the book. He had started a teaching career in Greenland, with an education in teaching from the Greenlandic Seminary and Tønder Seminary in South Jutland to draw upon. He lived up to the expectations that were made of him. Nielsen has, through his work in the school system and in the service of information—most recently as the leader of Greenland's radio—always had a connection to the cultural concept. Through his books, articles and lectures, he has interpreted the cultural heritage from the Eskimoic ancestors, and he is an eager proponent of contact with kinsmen in Canada.

Frederik Nielsen has simultaneously presented himself as a facilitator of the cultural influence from Denmark, among other things through his translations of the works of Danish authors—H. C. Andersen's fairy tales, the psalms of Grundtvig, The Fishermen by Hans Kirk—to mention a few. Frederik Nielsen has furthermore contributed in making Greenland's cultural situation known to Danish readers through a series of articles, e.g. in the "Greenland" journal.

In 1972, Frederik Nielsen was awarded the honorary award of the Greenlandic Society, the Rink medal. An account was made on this occasion of Nielsen's efforts in the field of culture.

The poems of Frederik Nielsen are among the most cherished and most sung in Greenland. Among these is the poem *"Panna qilassuaq allaaqqivissoq"* about the beautiful Greenlandic nature. Here is the poem as translated by Mads Lidegaard:

1)
Far above the earth, the bluing sky
arches above my head like a roof.
Out across the land the flowers' throng
broadly, like a blanket on a midsummer day.
The straws of the heather field
the little flowers
spice the fell-land air with pleasant smells.

2)
The towering snow-clad peaks of the fells
eternal world that never perishes
calmly they lie in the sun and shine
far up where meddling fingers cannot reach.
Perfectly calm water
Icebergs at the beach
Become a beautiful painting before my eyes.

3)
I hear the winged flocks daily
like an orchestra from the king's chapel
the twittering of finches from the
dwarf willow answers
sounds out around the house from morning
until evening.

Away we go,
a wheatear beats
the time with his tail, like a fine conductor.

4)
And on the top of a fell in the quiet evening
I often listen to the song of the birds
involuntarily clap in time with the beats
caught by the polyphonic tones of
the long-tailed duck.
Do as I do
hurry through!
Come to hear the play of the hues.

5)
Life is wonderful, and I could never
swap my country and its teeming flora
the animals, the flowers, the fjords and sounds,
the white fells and the choirs of birds.
Swap with you?
Oh no you don't!
Never will I swap for anything on earth.

Preface

The Arctic explorer Knud Rasmussen has taken an interest in and supported the nascent Greenlandic authors. This is apparent from Knud Rasmussen's letter of recommendation to the Greenland Administration, which can be read here:

To the Greenland Administration.

In the North Greenland Mail this year, I have been sent a manuscript: *Tumarse kinguaringnik oqalugtuaq*, from a teacher at the continuation school in Egedesminde, Frederik Nielsen, with a request to get it printed through the Greenlandic Literary Society.

Following a very thorough review of manuscript, I thus permit myself to address the Administration with an enquiry as to whether it might be possible to have the book brought out in the same way that Avggo Lynge's book was in its time.

Frederik Nielsen's book can be characterized as a family drama, which begins far up in Northern Greenland at a time where Christianity hadn't yet fully penetrated. Because of a blood feud, Tumarse's family move south and the plot then takes place at a particular hunting settlement – with the depiction of life, both at sea hunting for seals, as well as in the fjords hunting for caribou.

A curse from the time of the blood feud rests upon the family, whose best male elements all perish kayaking. These events are naturally and effectively depicted by the author, who, in contrast with his colleagues: Storch and Lynge, who have both addressed the future Greenland, has provided an unusually pretty depiction of the old Greenlandic society, with its joys and its tragedies.

The disposition of the entire book is built up by an artist who seems possessed of good literary abilities, but at no point does he misuse his ability. He has, on the contrary, understood how to add true Greenlandic color and atmosphere to his prose. The modern narrator has, first and foremost, acquired the tone of the legends, which repeatedly breaks through in realistic depictions.

I do not hesitate in describing the book as a significant work. I am convinced that the Administration would gain great benefit, should a printing be decided upon this year.

Respectfully
Knud Rasmussen
The North Sea,
29th June 1933

Glossary

Ammassat (singular ammassak) – small, vitamin-rich, salmon fish, which are called "lodder" in Danish, capelin in english.

Ammassivik (common place name) – a place where ammassat are gathered.

Atlatl - throwing wood, a tool with which to hurl harpoons.

Blue-side – a young harp seal. Grown it is called a black-side.

Catechist – teacher and preacher with training.

Colony manager – highest ranking official in a colony (town).

Fjord seal – a smaller type of seal, which is also called a ringed seal or net-side.

Half-fur – a short kayak fur which is attached around the kayak ring. It is used in calm weather.

Full-fur – a kayak fur which is tied tightly to the face, wrists and the kayak ring, so the hunter can turn in the water.

Ikerasassuaq (common place name) – broad and long sound.

Ilulissat (place name) – Jakobshavn, means "the ice fields."

Inspector – highest ranking official of the region.

Kayak ring – man hole in the kayak where the full and half furs are also attached.

Kangerlussuaq (common place name) – long fjord.

Naqerloq (place name) – hollow depression.

Qivittut (singular qivittoq) – Fell-walkers.

Reader – teacher and preacher without training.

Side room – an extension in the entrance passage.

Tuumarsi

Part One

I.

The north wind whistled through a cluster of small houses in Naqerloq. It was on such evenings that one really appreciated the comfort of indoors. And so it was in one of the houses. A wooden platter with cooked seal meat had been put to one side on the side-benches as a sign that the family had just eaten, and one could hear the dogs in the corridor crunching on some bones that had been thrown to them. The children had gone to bed and lay on the benches, while the adults sat, half-clad, on the edge of the benches, warm and full, and apparently without the desire to do anything.

A man of a ripe age sat on a chest—the traditional seat of the master of the house—and was gradually cutting away at an *atlatl*. But since the knife wouldn't really bite into it, he placed his work to one side, yawned, and said, "It would be nice to listen to a tale."

Some young heads suddenly popped up from beneath the blankets and began to shout in unison: "Tell us one, Grandma!"

From the furthest end of the bench-side came the voice of an old woman: "Now is the time to sleep. Sleep now, otherwise you will just oversleep tomorrow as usual."

"Please, Grandma, just one little story to fall asleep to," was the reply from the children.

"Oh, I know you; you won't relent until you have your way. But don't think I'm yielding to you by telling this story. I am only doing this because your father wants it."

"Wait a moment, mother, wait for me to lie down," said the master of the house, Tuumarsi. He hurriedly sorted out his things and signaled to his wife, who was sewing by the light.

Kaluliit—the lady of the house—put down her sewing without any rush. Then she sorted out the night-light and switched off the main light. She took some of her clothes off, pushed some of the children aside and lay down in her place next to her husband. The children, who had been squeezed together, began to fight to get more room. Their mother gently swatted the nearest ones and adjusted the blankets. Peace finally settled over the Tuumarsi family. Everyone had their allocated places on the benches.

Outside the north storm rushed forwards. And now that the house had gone quiet one could clearly hear how the snow heaped itself up against the window frames. Then the chanting tone was heard.

Once, many years ago, an umiak sailed into the fjord. It was people from the outer coast traveling in to their summer settlement. Late in the evening they laid to at a beach where the umiak could be drawn up onto land. They turned the umiak upside down and crawled underneath it to sleep.

They were woken from the middle of their sleep by a violent rushing noise from outside. What could that be? It couldn't be the wind, for it was not windy. The noise came in bursts, and each time almost lifted the umiak out of its supports. Everyone was gripped by fear, and even the men dared not crawl out to see what was wrong.

When it was finally over, they grew calmer. But suddenly they once more heard a scary sound, a shout of fear as if from someone buried alive. A terrible fear once more gripped the people under the umiak, and they crawled around trying to hide behind each other.

Among them was an orphaned boy. He was of course also afraid and tried to hide himself somewhere, but cowed as he was, he didn't dare mingle with the others. When the scary noise had passed, one could hear the whispering of an old woman, who was known for practicing witchcraft: "Someone wants to take one of us. There is no doubt. Push the orphan out; he's useless anyway." In that same moment the scary noise returned, closer than before. And when everyone, shouting and screaming, demanded that the boy be thrown out, one of the men pushed him outside and then knocked over the supports, so the umiak sealed itself completely around them. And in so doing the scary noise also ended.

The people in the umiak did not dare stay any longer. In the middle of the night they left, without any thought for the fate of the poor orphaned boy.

They had a wonderful time at their summer settlement. It was as if the scary experience had been forgotten. Wasn't it just a dream? You experience so many strange things which you forget the next day, or at a later time. But this experience was probably harder to forget. For they no longer had the orphaned boy with them. But on the other hand, there were so many ways to vanish, and they knew that.

One evening the sky grew suddenly dark, and the rain began to pour down. People stayed inside their tent, and settled down earlier than they usually would. Suddenly a rushing sound could be heard, which grew stronger and stronger as it approached the tent, and finally it grew so strong that the tent was almost pulled up. People were terrified, and crawled around amongst one another. When things finally grew quiet, a whispering and a stomping could be heard outside the tent, and its inhabitants were struck dumb with fear, while they resisted weeping to avoid giving away their presence. They heard the tent flap be shaken violently, and through a crack created by this, they heard someone whisper:

"We have come from afar. You won't let us lie in peace in our graves. We gave you a scare, but that seemingly wasn't enough."

Steps were heard behind the tent. And then could be heard: "Let us wait a bit. It won't stop raining right away, and it is a long time until dawn. Let us take it easy."

The inhabitants of the tent couldn't move for sheer fear. And the most terrified ones were the male head of the family and his mother, the woman who was known for her witchcraft.

The rain came down more heavily than before. A rushing sound could be heard, like that of a storm, and sometimes scary noises and voices could be heard too, as if from a partially strangled throat. The steps approached the entrance to the tent from both sides, and as the tent flap was pushed to one side, the following words were heard:

"Let witches and murderers come out to their victims. If that does not happen, you will all die of fear."

The tent was filled with screams and weeping, and the inhabitants fought to evade the revenge of the spirits of the dead.

In the end they all lost consciousness.

The day dawned with fine weather, and the sunshine peeked in through the opening of the tent flap and woke the unconscious people. Outside the tent flap lay the old woman, the witch, with bulging eyes, struck dead with fear. Her son was gone forever, as was his kayak.

The survivors hurriedly broke up their summer settlement, and they never returned.

Grandmother paused – she ended her story. In the silence afterwards, only snores could be heard. The children had already fallen asleep at the start of the tale.

"Ah," it came from the side where Tuumarsi lay. "I was almost about to fall asleep, but those damned witches kept me awake. Now we must sleep."

But grandmother could not sleep. It was always so when she had told stories of that type. Sleep had a hard time finding her when she remembered what had happened during her upbringing.

2.

Up north, somewhere in the Umanak Fjord, a little girl grew up under good conditions. Her father was one of the best hunters. She had a brother, older than her. She was fussed over a lot, as is often the case when a girl is named after a deceased sister.

She grew up without a care. She never noticed how sorrowful her father could become when he looked upon his children. She saw no particular reason to wonder why he made a special effort to teach her brother to hunt and use his strength.

The father, industrious as he was, was almost always away, and it was rare that he came home without a catch, even during times when game was scarce. He was a loner in several ways, and that was also noticeable in their family life. The house lay a good way away from the other houses, and they seldom visited anyone, and were rarely visited. The little girl was, at the time, so young as not to think anything of this.

It was clear in the little girl's memory that her mother had died suddenly. She also recalled wondering why her father gradually lost interest, so to speak, in everything, even in his profession of hunting. His only interest was the care of his son.

The little girl missed her mother a lot, and the fellowship of her brother was almost the only thing to give her pleasure. The brother had now grown so big that he could go hunting, and he always went with his father when he could get his act together enough to go out. The girl had reached the age when she started to notice what happened around her, and it was noticeable to her that both her father and brother had grown more and more serious. Or was it just her imagination?

She did not completely lack company, as they lived with two of her father's sisters, both widows. But of course they could not replace a mother. Nor did they do much to divert their niece; they probably had other things to consider.

One day the father left for the market and did not return at the time he'd usually be expected. The son had come home from the hunt, and he stood watch all night, waiting for his father. At dawn he leapt up and lashed out with balled fists and screamed madly:

"Just you wait. You have killed my father while he was alone, but more shall fall to my vengeance!"

He threw himself down on the benches and slept through the entire day. The next day they broke up camp and moved to a different settlement.

Only then did the little girl understand what had concerned her father.

At the time when the little girl had grown into a young girl, her brother came home from a hunting trip without a catch. He ordered a quick breaking of camp. The umiak was made ready, and they left and simply rowed and rowed south. Only two days later did they seek a tent site.

The family was fleeing from a double murder. The girl's brother had picked out a father and son—whom he believed to be his father's murderers—to be the victims of his vengeance. He made his preparations a long time beforehand. He had given himself plenty of time. Time and time again he had hidden at the end of a headland that he knew his enemies must pass on their way to and from their settlement. The execution of the plan had needed to be delayed many times due to various reasons, such as wind and weather and the presence of accompanying kayaks. But one day it succeeded.

They continued their journey south and settled in the vicinity of Ilulissat.

The wife to the murdered man had practiced witchcraft in order to revenge herself upon the murderer of her husband and son, as well as his family, wherever they might be. In a roundabout way, she let her curses be known:

"Give them my regards and tell the murderer of my husband and son, and his family, that they will perish in the sea."

Even after the baptism, and inclusion into the Christian church, the girl had trouble forgetting these words, but she comforted herself that such things belonged to the heathens, and that it did not apply to the believers.

The years passed at the new settlement, and she grew up. She met a young hunter from the southern part of the country, and the acquaintance resulted in marriage. Once more she had to move. They had three children, but only the oldest, Tuumarsi, reached adulthood. She again experienced a great sorrow when her husband perished during a sudden storm, and later she heard that her brother had fallen through the ice and had frozen to death.

Grandmother hid the vengefulness in her heart. She had never opened up to anyone, and would never do so, so long as she felt able to endure life's vicissitudes alone.

3.

Tuumarsi woke at daybreak. While the others slept, he got up and looked out. It was still blowing quite a bit, but the weather was clear. While he was getting dressed, the women awoke and began to stir.

Tuumarsi left the house towards where his kayak lay on the frame. While he stood there looking at the weather, lights shone in the houses. The men would soon be on their way to their kayaks. Shortly after, they all stood together at the usual gathering point.

"It seems like it won't subside for the time being," said Abili and knocked his feet together a few times in order to get some warmth into them.

"However, it isn't blowing as much as last night, and if it stays clear, then it might be worth a try," replied Ujuaannaat.

"Regardless of that, there are enough seals,"

said Tuumarsi, "at least there were yesterday. Perhaps we should give it a try."

"It is still early in the day, let us get a measure of the weather. The wind may easily turn when it grows lighter," said Abili.

Suddenly a coughing sound was heard, followed by spitting. This was Giitioorsuaq, an older hunter, who had almost become a landlubber. But he still trooped up every time the hunters made preparations for their hunting trips.

For a long time he looked at the weather. "As things look at the moment it can't get worse," he said. "I have certainly told Aggu, that there is no reason to stay at home when a good catch is waiting out there. I expect him to go."

Shortly after, the hunters parted and went home.

Tuumarsi and Giitioorsuaq remained behind and studied the weather more closely. Tuumarsi spoke of his hunting trip the previous day, then went home. After having drunk his morning coffee, he prepared to set off. Other hunters had either got into their kayaks, or were in the process of carrying them down to the beach.

After the father left, the children awoke and immediately started eating yesterday's leftover seal meat. When they had eaten, their mother told them to get up.

The bedclothes were stacked against the wall. Grandmother took off her kamiks, retired to the benches and began to soften a Fjord seal skin which was to be used to make kamik socks. Kaluliit took care of the smallest children and simultaneously took care of the seal meat which, along with the blubber-filled seal-stomachs, were to be stored in the storehouse. She grumbled from time to time when she couldn't get any peace and quiet from the smallest children.

"You," she said to one of her daughters, "bring the seal meat and the blubber out to the storehouse. Remember to close the door properly so the dogs can't get in. Ujuaannaat, go outside instead of loitering in here. It is fine weather to be out in, the other boys are probably already out. Iisaaq, bring that piece of meat to Michael's house and say that we didn't get round to bringing any out yesterday, as it had grown too late. Hurry now."

The oldest of the boys, Timuutu, came in and insisted on going kayaking, as the weather had improved. His grandmother beat his mother to it and replied in a sharp tone:

"Do you remember what your father said? You can only go kayaking with him. Without his permission, you cannot."

"Oh, it's so boring to walk around at home without anything to do. If only I had asked father if I could go out with him."

"Take your brother grouse hunting. It is said that there are many of them on the other side of the fell," said his mother.

"Grouse?" said Timuutu, "that's not for me."

"Then go outside instead of standing around babbling," said his mother.

The wind quieted as it grew lighter. When the hunters reached their hunting areas, it was almost calm.

Seals popped up here and there, but they

didn't stay up long enough for the hunters to get close to them. The entire morning passed without a catch. Towards the afternoon, Tuumarsi managed to harpoon a blue-side *(see glossary)*. He prepared it for towing and was soon on his way home. The other hunters stayed in their hunting areas in order to try their luck for a little longer.

As it grew dark all the hunters had come home, some with a catch. Aggu was one that had caught a whopper of a blue-side, so Giitioorsuaq need not go without fresh meat for a few days. He always said that he preferred death to going without seal meat.

Overall, the inhabitants of Naqerloq had nothing to complain about. The weather was unstable, as the transition from autumn to winter usually was, but no worse than that the hunters were still able to get out and obtain food for not only the same day, but also the subsequent days. It was not necessary to start eating into the winter stores.

In Tuumarsi's home, fresh seal meat was cooked, enough for visitors to also partake in the meal. Then it was time to go to bed after a good day, and with good expectations for the next.

4.

Naqerloq was a relatively new settlement. Not many people lived there at the beginning, but the place gradually grew as more and more people moved from poorer hunting sites to the good one. However, it was not all newcomers that stayed at Naqerloq. Some broke up after just a single winter and moved to other places. The reason for these moves was, among other things, that some thought Naqerloq was too far away from the nearest trading post, and that the sailing route between them could be tricky, not least during winter.

The first to settle at Naqerloq were the Tuumarsi and Giitioorsuaq families. The latter was a kind of "elder" at the site, since he was the oldest.

The settlement carried with it changes and deprivations, not least for Tuumarsi's mother. What she missed most was the Service on Sundays with bell ringing and psalm singing. She tried to preserve that Sunday tradition by getting up early and making morning coffee for the others. When the time approached 10, she rushed to get her Sunday clothes on—even though there really was no reason to rush—and then pretended that she couldn't find her psalm book. She was opposed to people going out hunting on a Sunday. Tuumarsi liked to comply with his mother's wishes, but it was hard for him to stay home when he knew there was a good catch to be had. He would then leave in the afternoon, when the prayers at the reader's house were over.

Keeping Sundays holy was an ingrained custom in Tuumarsi's childhood home. They had lived at a place with a church building, and Tuumarsi himself liked to be in church with his father and mother. But the place had not been a good hunting site, and when Tuumarsi reached the age where he could handle himself as an independent hunter, he often advocated that it would be best to move to a better hunting site. At that time his father was inexorable. Tuumarsi later understood that his father's resistance was due to him wanting to be in a place with a church. But there had been several incidents in Tuumarsi's childhood that had led him to wonder about his father's view.

His father never went hunting on a Sunday, and he stuck to that regardless of whether they had food or not. When his son wept from hunger in the morning, he comforted him by telling him that he should wait in confidence that God would give them something to eat. And when someone came and gifted them presents of meat, Tuumarsi always thought that it was a gift from God to reward those people who obeyed His commandment of keeping the day holy.

One Sunday morning—Tuumarsi must have been about 10 years old at the time—he had woken and felt the hunger gnawing. He had known that there was no food in the house, as his father hadn't caught anything for several days. He wept and wept, but in the end let himself be comforted by the usual words from his father.

In the afternoon, he left their house and met Abili, who had come with a proper hunk of meat. "This is for you," Abili said, "my father has caught a seal. He left this morning and returned just after the service."

"Have other hunters been out?"

"Oh yes, almost all of them. How can it be that your father is never out on a Sunday? He could have caught a seal just like the rest."

Tuumarsi had walked on with confused thoughts. Yes, how could it be that his father never went out on a Sunday, when all the other hunters could, and yet still come back with a catch? But he had trouble concentrating on it, for he was constantly thinking of the fact that his mother was in the process of cooking seal meat back home. He tried to stay out a little longer, but in the end he had to hurry home–the thought of meat had grown unbearable to resist.

5.

He entered the ranks of the adults and became a hunter, but his lifestyle did not change because of it. He lived as he had been raised to. He held fast to his esteem for his parents, and he would not deviate from this principle. He had his own ideas regarding how a hunting family ought to adapt to ensure their existence, ideas that were not in harmony with his father's. But he never uttered these thoughts, to avoid hurting him. He still had to put up with staying at home on Sundays.

It didn't mean as much now because there were two providers, and during the good hunting times they caught so much that they didn't need to go without anything, and there were always plenty of winter stores. Tuumarsi's mother had more than enough to do. It ended with Tuumarsi marrying. The chosen girl was from a settlement that lay nearby.

His marriage meant no change for their family life. Tuumarsi respected his father as head of the family, even if he might wish for greater independence.

Then one day it happened that the hunters were surprised by a violent storm. Tuumarsi was one who managed to save himself, but his father was among those that perished. It was a hard blow for the family, not least for Tuumarsi's mother. The sorrow had been so crushing that she grew ill and lay for a long time on her bed on the benches. When Tuumarsi regained his senses after this, he felt like a grown man for the first time—a feeling he hadn't had even after he got married. He was now the only provider for the family. He would have to handle his tasks as the head of the family by keeping a hold of traditions and respecting the family life, just as his father had wanted it to be. He even begrudged himself for ever having had differing thoughts with regards to what was best for the family.

"God, give me strength for my work. Help me follow in my father's footsteps, give me the power to help my family, so they do not suffer want . . . yes, do not suffer want." He repeated those words time and time again, as if he wanted to imprint their meaning upon himself.

When he sat at his mother's bedside and saw how hard the sorrow had hit her and how much she suffered inside, he promised to keep and abide by the promise he made.

6.

When sorrow's paralyzing blow has been overcome, and normal life presents itself with demands for existence, it can be difficult to keep one's good resolutions. It is the fight for existence which is the deciding factor when you want to survive. So it is with a hunting people, at last.

Tuumarsi reluctantly had to acknowledge this. The place where they lived had never been a good hunting site. More and more newcomers arrived, so more and more needed to feed themselves by hunting. In other words, there were now too many hunters in relation to the amount of available game. People heard of other places where there were plenty of all kinds of game. The thought of moving to such a place had become an obsession with Tuumarsi.

When Tuumarsi announced that they had to move to another place, his mother was very much against the idea. She didn't want to go without a Service in a real church. As always it was hard for Tuumarsi to contradict his mother, but on this point he pressed. He also had to think of his boy's upbringing and training in the hunting profession.

One spring day he came back from his hunting trip without a catch. When "Umiak" was shouted, he went down to the beach in a dejected mood. His mood did not improve when he saw that the umiak was full of large quantities of meat, blubber and skins. Such a wealth! And he himself had been out all day and returned empty-handed: this was to be the end of the wretched hunting life in this place!

He wandered around for a long time in order to organize his confused thoughts. When he finally decided upon what he wanted to say to his household, he went home. As he entered the entrance passage there was a smell of cooked seal meat. Oh, so they were cooking seal meat, a gift, not my catch! Full of shame and anger, he stormed in, went over to the stove without a word, picked up the pot with both hands and poured the entire contents out in the entrance passage. The dogs gained an unexpected feast.

The women burst into hysterical weeping, they had never experienced Tuumarsi behaving in such a way. Then the children also began to cry. Without a word Tuumarsi took his hunting implements and left the house. He took his kayak down off its frame, carried it down to the beach and left.

He was still wrought. His mood had not improved, in his anger, by pouring the contents of the pot out in the entrance passage. The hysterical weeping of the women did not affect him. He was possessed of one single thought, and that was to move some place else in the summer, as early as possible. He had now made the final decision of breaking away from the existence he had been raised to live in.

He only calmed down when he caught a seal. But it was not long before he felt pangs of remorse. He repented for having acted rashly.

His fellow residents were probably now busy talking.

When he laid to at the beach with his catch, there was nobody to receive him. Slowly he walked up towards their house, and when he came in, everyone had already gone to bed. The house was sad and cold. Full of shame, he undressed and laid himself down in his place. It was impossible for him to fall asleep. At daybreak he got up and once more went hunting. He wanted to have plenty of time to think everything through and then come home as early as possible. He caught a seal early on in the day and rowed home. As soon as he came into the house he sat down on his usual seat. Then he tearfully unburdened his heart to his mother and his wife, who wept quietly while they listened to his words.

Peace returned to the family.

In the evening Grandmother whispered to her daughter-in-law: "Kaluliit, we must now be prepared to move come summer."

That Sunday Tuumarsi went to church and sat down at the very last bench in the back. He felt as if everyone was looking at him.

7.

Tuumarsi for a while had a place in mind, where, in his opinion, there was good hunting. It was there he moved the family at the start of the summer, accompanied by Giitioorsuaq and his family. Before this Tuumarsi had—primarily for his mother's sake—had a talk with their catechist about how things might be arranged with regards to services and potential education of the children at the new site.

"Oh, so you intend to move?" the catechist said. "What does your mother say to that?"

The catechist was an older man, trained by a priest called Kjer, something he often brought about. In a show of respect for his old teacher, he started every service with one of his psalms.

"Yes, we are moving," Tuumarsi replied. "The hunting around here isn't good enough when one needs to subsist on one's catch."

"Yes," the catechist continued, "so it goes, as it says in the Scripture: The world and its glory are coming to an end. What does your mother say to moving?"

"She wasn't much in favor of it. She is, of course, quite old. But now she agrees on the matter."

"We will miss your mother at our services," the catechist said, and continued: "See, Tuumarsi. What you did to your mother that time in the spring . . . the sorrow you caused her, is highly lamentable. Do not let it happen again. You have probably noticed for yourself how the congregation that was gathered in the church directed their gazes at you. I have long wanted to speak to you about it . . . and I have finally now been given the opportunity."

"My mother and I have talked about it and have come to a good understanding with each other. It was regrettable that I participated in the service that Sunday," Tuumarsi continued with a sudden irritation, "and disturbed the service."

The catechist realized that they were about to broach a dangerous subject. He could not afford to insult Tuumarsi, who was always generous towards them when it came to gifts of meat. It was best to change the subject.

"Yes, yes . . . but you asked who might conduct the service?"

"Yes, it certainly won't be me, being unworthy of preaching god's word," Tuumarsi replied. He regretted the words he'd said to the catechist in his irritation, and continued: "But I hope I can somehow be of use."

The catechist did not want to make a decision; he had to speak to the priest first, he said. —"Besides, it is said you have caught another seal. It seems you are the only one catching anything."

Tuumarsi left. He smiled at the thought that he had dared—in irritation, admittedly—counter the catechist when the latter had tried to censure him for his behavior.

"Yes," he thought to himself, "the catechist didn't really dare chastise me. He is probably reluctant to go without the good pieces of meat that we give him. True, I acted very rashly in the spring, but I do not like to be reminded of it."

"Send some delicious seal meat to the catechist's place," he told his wife when he came home. "Ideally, more than usual, you never know when they will get any again."

8.

Giitioorsuaq was appointed as "reader" in Naqerloq. Tuumarsi's mother had wished for her son to be reader, thinking Giitioorsuaq was not really suited to conducting the Service. He was incapable of leading a song, and as soon as he made preparations to do so, the congregation would chime in with Tuumarsi's mother as lead singer. Giitioorsuaq's attempts at drowning them out never amounted to much.

The task of a reader was to teach children. The "education" took place in Giitioorsuaq's house. First and foremost the children had to learn to read, and in that regard the larger children knew more than their "teacher." All the children would, in unison, read the same pieces again and again, to their great amusement. When Giitioorsuaq's wife was in a bad mood, which was often due to the absence of the life-giving morning coffee, and told off the children, they would rush out of the house and amuse themselves while listening to the quarrel inside.

Back at home, Tuumarsi did his best to take care of the children's education in Christianity. In the evening, when there was peace in the house, he would read with them, primarily the Lord's prayer and the creed. During these devotional evenings, he felt the joy of family life, but he could simultaneously not avoid feeling burdened by his responsibility.

At the start of the next wintering year, the proper Sunday prayers were over. Giitioorsuaq had so much pain in one leg that he had to remain bedridden most of the time. People made do with gathering to sing psalms and occasionally praying from time to time. When the priest came to their place on his tour over the summer, he encouraged Tuumarsi to become reader, which Tuumarsi had to decline, as he still felt that he wasn't suitable for it. The priest promised to obtain a suitable man from outside.

9.

The priest was true to his promise. A hunter by the name of Andariarsi moved to Naqerloq at the request of the priest. One Saturday, early in the autumn, the catechist in Ikerasassuaq came to install the new reader. This was to happen the following day, Sunday.

The day dawned with fine weather. Of course nobody was going hunting that day. The festively dressed people were out and about from the early morning onwards.

The service was to happen in the open. The congregation was assembled on a small plateau in front of a mountain slope. Slightly before ten o'clock the catechist came out of his tent with the bible under his arm, followed by the new reader Andariarsi, who looked very serious.

The service began with the catechist's favorite psalm. He stood before the congregation, made a prayer and read a text from Jesus' sermon on the mount.

His main theme were the words: "Seek first his kingdom and his righteousness, and all these things will be given to you as well." (Matthew 6:33) One might say that people haven't made an effort to keep these words in mind over recent years. People are first and foremost interested in worldly things, and think that those that belong to the kingdom of God come second. For example, we see a lot of hunters go hunting on Sunday, paying no heed to the summons of the church bell. They should know that God will not let them want the necessities of life, when he provides food to the birds of the sky. He hopes that the population of this place will keep God's word in mind and keep Sunday holy, and not let themselves be led by concerns about worldly, corruptible things.

His audience listened quietly and reverently, with only the cries of the infants breaking the silence. This, however, did not seem to bother the catechist. He grew so heated in his speech that the sweat dripped down from his chin.

In the end, he announced that Andariarsi was now employed as the site's reader, and Andariarsi grew red faced when everyone looked towards him. Then the catechist thanked the site's outgoing reader for his good work among the congregation.

At these words the audience shot glances in all directions. It was as if they were searching for something. Where was Giitioorsuaq? He was not there. And while the catechist was seemingly occupied with his own thoughts, a woman was clearly heard whispering:

"Where is Giitioorsuaq?"

The catechist said amen, and the service ended, but people's minds were mostly occupied by the absence of Giitioorsuaq.

Shortly after the service, Giitioorsuaq came home with a seal in tow. Since his son Aggu had stayed at home, he had borrowed his kayak and had gone out to obtain some fresh meat for the catechist. He had felt like going on a small kayak trip after such a long period of inactivity due to illness, and it was such wonderful weather.

Even his wife had not known that he had gone out hunting. She gave him a real earful: he should be ashamed of himself. He knew that the catechist was to conduct a service. It was clear why he was being set aside as reader, such an ungodly oaf, who didn't even bother taking part in the service on Sunday. He hadn't even heard the catechist thanking him, which he hadn't deserved anyway, such an old landlubber, who had snuck away just to try being his own master. He certainly shouldn't expect her to flense his wretched catch.

Giitioorsuaq didn't bother replying. He felt true hunter's pride. He still had it, the old man! He had lain down for most of the year, and now he had taken the opportunity, while all the hunters had stayed at home, to show his ability, even if it was in a borrowed kayak!

When his wife paused her tirade to catch her breath, he whispered to his daughter-in-law:

"Suusaat, my catch is lying down on the beach. Go down and flense it, the catechist should ideally eat fresh meat."

It seemed that the catechist didn't know what had actually happened. He was invited to eat seal meat with Giitioorsuaq, and when he was informed that it was Giitioorsuaq's catch that he was eating he was very impressed and commended him for still being able to make a catch. He didn't ask when he had caught the seal. The way Giitioorsuaq's wife talked, the others didn't have a chance to get a word in.

10.

A summer had once more come to an end, and the residents of Naqerloq prepared for yet another winter. In addition to the new reader and his family, a lot of hunting families had arrived, attracted by the rumors of good hunting conditions. Among the newcomers was Tuumarsi's brother-in-law and his family. Since they hadn't had the time to build a house of their own, they took up lodgings at Tuumarsi's place. The brother-in-law was a skilled hunter.

The hunters made use of every opportunity to go hunting. But it did happen that they had to remain at home when it was too stormy. The best hunting areas were by the outer coast, towards the open sea. But as soon as the weather was good enough to go out in, they caught so much that they didn't need to rely on their winter stores.

In the beginning of the fourth wintering year the hunters had a premonition that it would be a bad winter for hunting. The weather was very unstable, with changing winds and with prolonged westerly storms from time to time. For it is of course the case that the westerly storms push the ice inwards, so it blocks the exit routes to the hunting areas. And when this happens there isn't much to do other than wait for the wind to switch to the north east and drive the ice back out. At the same time these winds arrive with a sudden ferocity, accompanied by snowfall. When the hunters study the weather in the morning and, from the air temperature, the clouds, the colors in the sky and the direction of the wind, can conclude that a westerly storm is brewing, they prefer to stay at home. When you go hunting after such a storm has finished, then it is as if the sea has been swept clean of game.

This winter was the worst so far. They would have been in great distress, had they not secured plenty of winter stores. There were, however, some that hadn't done so, in the belief that there would, as usual, be enough game to find. They only made it through the winter with the help of others. When the weather grew more stable towards the end of the winter, the game animals returned, and one catch after another was brought home. Those who had previously decided to move spoke of it no more.

When the routes out to the hunting areas were either blocked by ice, or there was no hunting to be had, the hunters stood idly at their usual gathering place. In normal circumstances they would mostly talk about their experiences during the hunt, but now they almost exclusively spoke about the weather and the absence of game. Tuumarsi used any opportunity to remind the others that this winter should be a lesson to all. "We have always known that one can never say anything for certain about how a winter will run. We similarly know that the hunting opportunities are reduced everywhere during winter, and that the game may stay away for shorter or longer periods. This is why you need to remember the old rule: to collect plenty of winter supplies during the summer, while there is plenty to catch. We must always imagine the winter as being a time when there is nothing to catch. What would happen if we didn't have enough winter stores? Those who have not managed to gather enough supplies must learn the lesson of the winter we just experienced."

"Recriminations are pointless," said Piitrusi, "We were made to believe that Naqerloq was a place where the hunting opportunities never failed, even during winter. We moved here because we believed what had been said of the place."

"Did anyone encourage you to come here? Hmm . . . Hmm . . . it certainly wasn't one of us that did so," Giitioorsuaq grumbled, who wouldn't tolerate people speaking disparagingly of the place that he had helped found.

"Yes, yes," Piitrusi replied, "if you don't want us here, then we'll move in summer. You are so miserly, you'd begrudge us simply for living here."

"Had we been miserly, where would you be? You'd probably be lying on the benches,"

Aggu said, insulted on his father's behalf.

Tuumarsi tried to smooth over the embarrassing situation that had arisen from this exchange. One should not misconstrue his words. He did not wish to insult anyone, but simply wanted to point out how crucial it was to gather sufficient winter supplies.

"In these difficult times we must support one another and consider winter supplies common property. That is an old rule, which is still valid in a hunting community," he added.

On his way home, Tuumarsi pondered the situation further, and had to admit to himself that he wouldn't mind if some of the families left Naqerloq. He predicted that there could be some long-term difficulties providing enough food for so many people. This problem worried him.

II.

Spring and summer came again, with plenty of game. The hunting families that had spoken of moving the previous winter had apparently given up on their plans to do so.

The hunters brought back one catch after another, and it was a busy time for the women who took care of the handling and preparation of the catches. The meat that was left over from the daily housekeeping was to be hung up to dry. The blubber had to be filled into blubber bags, but most of it was to be stored in order to be later transported for sale at the trading post. The skins had to be processed, both for home use and for sale. Blubber and skins were the only trade goods, and for the money earned, necessary and indispensable shop items were to be purchased. The spring ammassat catch had started, and provided a plentiful winter store of the dried little fish. Taught by experience, Tuumarsi and a couple of other level-headed men reminded their fellow residents of the necessity of collecting sufficient winter stores.

During the previous winter some of the hunters had had the idea that it would be nice to have either a shop or just a depot of the most necessary shop items on site. The wish was motivated by the long distance from Naqerloq to the trading post, which could also be quite difficult to sail to during the winter due to the ice blockage. The idea gained broad support, and people agreed to put the case before the colony manager. Tuumarsi was chosen to be speaker, and for the execution of the mission he chose the most appropriate time for himself. They were, at this time, just about to go ammassat catching in the fjord, and the umiak with his family accompanied him for much of the way, before he, in his kayak, set a course for the colony site.

He looked forward to seeing the place again, for it was a long time since he had been there. There were, after all, a lot of old acquaintances that he wanted to say hello to.

With rising waters, he rowed between the many small islands. On one of them lay the colony site. Around him boys rowed in kayaks

—budding hunters—who practiced throwing harpoons or bird spears. He came to think of his own boys. They were also at the practicing stage, but they had their playground in far more troubled waters.

He was received by a dear old acquaintance. Just as entered the house that he was to live in, messages came with invitations from various families.

The next day he went to speak with the colony manager, whom he knew beforehand. He was not entirely unawed, however. It was not normal for a Greenlander to so readily address a Danish official. But the colony manager received him warmly.

Without any preamble, Tuumarsi put forth the wish of the settlement and the reasons behind it.

The colony manager smiled at first, without saying anything. He was so used to receiving requests of this type. His smile spurred Tuumarsi to greater efforts.

"After what we experienced last winter, we thought it would be reassuring to have a little shop. Under normal conditions we catch so many seals that we have an abundance of blubber, far more than we have any opportunity to sell, as the way to the nearest trading post is long, and because it can be hard to travel in an umiak, especially in rough seas."

The colony manager asked how many people lived in Naqerloq, and how many seals were caught over the course of a year, as an estimate, and he continued:

"I can understand your motivations for having a shop. But on the other hand one has to consider that Naqerloq is a relatively new place, and we do not yet have any basic experiences with regards to the stability of the hunting potential and the population. As one of the reasons for your request, you have indicated that the hunting potential can fail, which has also happened. And it is exactly that which gives us some misgivings about accommodating your wish."

Tuumarsi didn't quite understand this at first. But after the colony manager had elaborated, he could only agree with his arguments.

"You are not alone in wanting a shop," the colony manager continued, "I get this wish from all small settlements. But it must be obvious to anyone that we cannot supply every place with a shop or depot."

"I am not talking about the other places," Tuumarsi replied. "I speak on behalf of our own settlement, as one of the first settlers."

The colony manager brought forth further explanations. It was, incidentally, a case that he would have to present to the inspector, who made decisions of this type. The population of Naqerloq would of course be informed of the outcome of the case, but when, he couldn't say for certain. He categorically turned down the establishment of a depot.

That day Tuumarsi stayed at the colony site. The next day, early in the morning, he was on his way to Ammassivik. When they couldn't get a shop, they would necessarily have to ensure their existence by collecting winter stores even more than ever.

12.

In Ammassivik there were happy days. As usual there were many people who had come from both near and far to gather ammassat and catch the seals that followed their shoals. At the ebb, ammassats were scooped up with home made rackets made from skin. The catch was carried up and spread out on flat sloped rocks to dry. People cooked meat, fish and made coffee, games and competitions were organized and there was dancing in the evening. Everyone enjoyed life in the open after being pent up in their small winter houses.

For some reason Tuumarsi felt at ease and was in a good mood. Granted, he had decided what he wanted to say when he arrived at Ammassivik, but he might as well make a bit of fun out of the result of his trip.

His settlement fellows were the first to greet him as he laid to at the beach. "What news, what news?" was shouted from all sides. Giitioorsuaq was there, and in his eagerness to move forward to be among the first to greet him, slipped and fell. This was greeted by mighty roars of laughter. With difficulty he got to his feet and scolded people left and right while he occasionally repeated: "What news? What news?"

"I am to pass on the regards of the colony

manager and say that the shop will be finished when you come home from catching ammassat," Tuumarsi shouted.

"What, what . . . what did he say," Giitioorsuaq asked eagerly, "what is the shop to . . . what is wrong with the ammassat catch . . . you wretched children, what are you doing here, get away from the beach, you are just taking up space. What did you say, Tuumarsi, did you say anything about the colony manager and about the shop, when . . . damned kids, get out of here, you're taking up the space of the elders . . . what was it you said Tuum . . . "

Tuumarsi had had enough fun now. He cut off Giitioorsuaq's flow of words by shouting:

"We won't get any shop this year. Naqerloq is too small to have a shop. It might first be considered in a couple of years."

That, at least, was a message that people could finally understand. Giitioorsuaq turned his face away from Tuumarsi and muttered: "What did I get out of that? Nothing more than a proper slide. If I ever meet the colony manager, I'll give him a piece of my mind. If only it had been me talking to him. Those damned Danes, only thinking about themselves. May they all soon travel home, the lot of them."

Other than that, Tuumarsi's message was received calmly by most. They knew that there had been wishes of this type from other places, and that they had not come to a good end. Even though they were disappointed, they downplayed it by making jokes regarding Giitioorsuaq's slip. They could have granted the colony manager the sight of that performance. It could have softened his heart and changed his mind, so he would give them a shop, wherein Giitioorsuaq could buy fabric for a new pair of trousers, and so forth.

But there were some who didn't like Tuumarsi, and to them the colony manager's refusal became a good weapon against him. They hinted that Tuumarsi pandered towards the Danes and wasn't the true representative for the inhabitants. It would have been better had they sent another, e.g. the reader, who without a doubt would have obtained a positive result.

Giitioorsuaq was disappointed, of course. He had so looked forward to going to the shop and buying tobacco. But he comforted himself with the fact that, if they couldn't get a shop this year, then it might be that they got one next year.

"You can wait as long as you like, it will only be after your death that Naqerloq gets a shop," said Piitrusi maliciously.

"You should probably go down to the beach and scoop up ammassat instead of standing around here idling, that way you'll have something to chew on this winter, when you're lying on the benches and don't have any food, other than that which you fantasize about," Aggu snapped back on his father's behalf.

"It may be a good thing that we don't get that shop," Piitrusi said evasively. "After all, it would just end up with you and Tuumarsi thinking it was yours, without giving the shop manager any say in the matter. The reader suggested that too."

"Those that have nothing to sell won't be allowed to buy anything either. What did you say about the reader?"

"You don't have to ask; you heard what I said."

"Let the reader choose his friends among his equals–bad hunters."

"Shh, shh, be quiet now, here comes the reader."

"Let him come," said Aggu, "I'll be sure to tell him what Piitrusi said."

Andariarsi smirked. "Ye-es, I hear that that thing with the shop wasn't possible. You don't always get what you want. It is said that the colony manager tends to be dismissive of certain people."

"We'll probably get over that. If we suffer want during the winter, we'll always be able to subsist on soporific sermons," Aggu said, then left, followed by his father and a few others.

Tuumarsi was in a good mood the entire evening. It seemingly didn't affect him when they told him about the embarrassing exchange. He would rather stay with his family, but since he knew that many wanted to hear news from the colony, he went out and headed towards a group of men that included Giitioorsuaq.

13.

One evening, in weather that was dead calm, the men, both the older and the younger ones, left in their kayaks to play and compete in harpoon throwing. Tuumarsi didn't go, as he preferred to be a spectator. He enjoyed the traditional performance and was simultaneously occupied in studying his son Timuutu's movements and technique.

In the middle of the games, the kayaks suddenly turned and headed outwards. It turned out that they had spotted a young seal. One might have thought that it was the first time they had seen such an animal, they were that eager to hit it. Then suddenly someone shouted that the seal should be killed with a bird spear. When the seal dived, the kayaks placed themselves in position and waited for it to reappear. As soon as it appeared as a black spot, bird spears were thrown from all sides, but it seemed that there was only one that hit its target. This turned out to be correct. When the kayaks reached the seal it lay there, struck and kept afloat by a single bird spear.

"That's my bird spear, my bird spear," people heard someone yell with a youthful voice. Everyone knew the voice; it was Timuutu's. Glowing red with pride, he took out his kayak knife and struck the killing blow to the seal.

Timuutu took the catch up onto his kayak and rowed home, accompanied by the others, who whooped and threw their spears around him in their joy. Before the group of kayaks completely reached the shore, the proud father shouted:

"There will be a manhood feast. Anyone who wants to come is welcome!"

Tuumarsi's invitation to communal eating was received with shouts of joy from all. It was clear that an event such as this was to be celebrated with a proper feast.

Seal meat was cooked in the pots of the Tuumarsi family until late into the night. Timuutu's catch, supplemented by pieces of meat from the contingency stores, vanished into the pots and were eaten up, after which coffee was served that was so strong that it laid itself like a membrane on the tongue. Such a repast was worthy of the event that had taken place, Tuumarsi thought, it was a good start to Timuutu's future career as a hunter.

A gathering such as this also had a reconciliatory significance and created unity. The two readers, the prior, Giitioorsuaq, and the present, Andariarsi, were comfortably chatting together as colleagues, even though Giitioorsuaq couldn't help but assert himself as elder, and thus most experienced. Aggu and Piitrusi were having great fun together and teased each other good-naturedly.

Only at dawn did silence settle over the camp. Snores and sounds of satiety could be heard from the tents. Only one man stood alone on the low fell, with folded hands, looking up to the sky with tears in his eyes.

"Thank you, God, thank you. You know why I thank you," he whispered.

The family must endure, and when it must endure there must be someone to facilitate its endurance. Tuumarsi had learned those words of wisdom from his father, but he had never quite understood their meaning until after his death. Now he was the facilitator, and he had to pass on that role to his sons.

14.

Later on that summer the Tuumarsi family went caribou hunting in Kangerlussuaq. He hadn't managed to go hunting the previous summer, so had decided to do it this year. His sons were so reluctant to miss out on it as well.

Timuutu was 16 years old, and had already started to catch seals from the kayak. The 13 year old Iisaaq had not yet reached that point, but he was practiced at hunting on land. Now they were on their way in through the fjord along with a couple of umiaks.

These were the well known reindeer hunting grounds! You could view it from a fell quite far from the coast. A broad valley led to an offshoot of the inland ice, surrounded by high fells, the high peaks of which seem to vanish into the blue-white inland ice. When one goes further in, large moraine mounds of clay and stone are visible. In the places where streams wind between smaller mounds the earth is covered by various types of lush vegetation. Further in is an extensive swampy area which is covered in heather on the more elevated parts. Reindeer cows graze with their calves between stone cairns on the mountainside, entirely preoccupied in eating. Reindeer bulls with towering antlers stand for a moment, scenting the air, before trotting over to a stream to slake their thirst.

Very early one morning, Tuumarsi set off along with his two sons and two women, who were traditionally employed as carriers. Tuumarsi walked sedately in front, with measured steps. The mosquitoes were already very bothersome, and from time to time he would brush his face to rid himself of them, and each time his palm would show completely black.

The sons followed next to one another, and in their eagerness and excitement they obviously didn't feel particularly bothered by the mosquitoes. They constantly spoke and had a hard time containing their excitement. Then they began to quarrel and argue, and when the youngest began to cry Tuumarsi had to intercede and threaten that, if he didn't stop crying, he wouldn't be allowed to take part in the actual hunting. Peace was quickly restored.

The women brought up the rear. They spoke softly to each other, and in spite of their burden they walked effortlessly and calmly. It was obvious that this wasn't the first time they were on such a trip.

When you need to walk all day without many rest breaks, then one must necessarily adapt accordingly. The leader must utilize the tactic learned from participating in the reindeer hunt as a youth. If the boys were to go in front, then one might expect them to either walk to fast, or to jog ahead without paying attention to their surroundings. That would result in them growing tired long before the end of the day, getting sore feet, taking too many rest breaks and drinking water each time they reach a stream. But when one has an experienced leader one needn't fear growing tired on the first day. And if ones feet grow sore, you can be sure that they will rest well overnight.

Tuumarsi was an experienced reindeer hunter, and thus also a practiced leader. He ignored the impatience of the boys and he plotted his route to give a wide berth at streams, so the boys were not tempted to drink water prematurely.

In the middle of the day, when the sun was at its highest, he stopped at the top of a hill and started to look around. With loud exclamations of tiredness, the boys threw themselves to the ground. The women placed their burdens down and sat without breaking off their conversation, seemingly unaffected by the trip. They merely stroked their foreheads at the place where the carrying straps had rested and they drew up their kamiks, which had begun to crease.

15.

Tuumarsi used his hand to shield his eyes and looked around. It wasn't long before he alerted the boys by pushing them in the direction of a valley that lay at the end of a pot-like stretch of swamp. The boys whispered "where, where," for they could see nothing apart from some large stones.

Only a practiced eye could see that there was something distinguishing itself from the large stones. And to an experienced reindeer hunter it was clear that it was a reindeer cow with two calves. Without waiting for the boys to spot them, the father got the boys to go forward with him while stooping. The wind direction was ideal. The boys instinctively understood that there was something ahead. Full of excitement they reached the top of a hill, and there the reindeer stood, a good distance away, peacefully grazing.

The boys were just about to charge forwards, but they were stopped by their father. There was a stretch yet to walk, still creeping, before they could get within firing range. Before they reached the top of the last hill, Tuumarsi ordered his boys to have their guns ready. The boys were to shoot the calf that kept itself furthest from its mother, while the father sought out the cow. No shots were to be fired until he gave the signal.

The boys aimed their guns and were ready

to shoot. A "bang" was heard suddenly, and the animals dashed off, scared by the shot.

Tuumarsi did not have time to yell at the boys. He quickly took aim and shot. The cow fell and stayed down. Next to him the boys were busy loading their guns while they argued. One accused the other of having fired too early.

"You certainly aren't easy to guide. Now hurry up and reload your guns and shoot at the calves. They will probably stay near their mother for a while," Tuumarsi said, before realizing he was alone. The boys had already dashed off after the animals. He recalled his first reindeer hunt and smiled.

The boys' hunting instinct could not be denied. They stopped a suitable distance from the animals, aimed, and shot at each of their prey. The calves fell, twitched a bit with their legs, then moved no more. The boys shouted with joy and ran towards them.

Tuumarsi slowly walked forward. He was completely satisfied with the boys' behavior. Yes, this had been one of his best experiences of a reindeer hunt. When there were two animals, then there was no question they took one each, but if there was one animal, then they would have zealously competed to be the first to fire, and they would have fallen out.

The boys lay on their stomachs and suckled the cow. They apparently knew in advance that that was what real reindeer hunters did. But with mock seriousness, their father roared at them:

"What are you doing to my animal? Go to your own!" The boys got up, laughing, and went over to the downed calves. They of course first had to investigate who had landed the best shot.

When the women arrived, they jointly began to cut up the animal. They extracted the most delicate parts to be their dinner and packed the rest of the meat in the skins and hid it between the rocks. Then they began to cook what they had brought. They ate, cooked again and ate again, until they couldn't eat more.

Tuumarsi found a suitable cave to spend the night in. They could only just fit there. Fragrant heather was spread across the ground as an underlay, and they laid themselves down with Tuumarsi closest to the entrance. As sated as they were, they soon fell asleep.

Early the next morning Tuumarsi woke his boys. They were to venture further inland. The women had already left with some of the catch from the previous day in order to bring to those remaining in the camp. They would return to the reindeer hunt later the same day.

16.

Tuumarsi and the boys wandered inland. They had now reached the real reindeer hunting grounds, and they took it easy. The plague of mosquitoes was worse than the previous day. The gentle morning wind from the inland ice was only short lived, and the place they were was so far inland that the breeze from the fjord couldn't reach it. This could be pretty rough, even for an experienced reindeer hunter.

There were a lot of reindeer in the hunting grounds. They could have downed as many as they wanted to, but Tuumarsi didn't want more at the moment. He knew where the reindeer bulls could be found, and those were his preferred prey.

In the middle of the day the heat grew almost intolerable, but they dared not take any clothes off due to the plague of mosquitoes. Then they took a break in a shady place and brought out the food bags. But the boys suddenly had the idea that they wanted to have something fresh to eat instead of yesterday's leftovers.

Their father gave them permission to shoot an animal or two, but simultaneously warned them against wasting the ammunition. This they promised. After a relatively short period of time, two shots rang out, and Tuumarsi went in the direction of the sound to see what was going on.

A reindeer cow and a calf lay on the ground. When their father reached the location, the boys suggested that they carry the entire animal to their resting place. Their father gave them permission to try.

The boys tried, in turns, to carry the reindeer cow on their backs, but after several attempts they had to give up. It was too heavy.

"Since you can't transport them as they are, we'd better stay here," said Tuumarsi. "When I was your age we could easily carry a reindeer cow, and carrying the calves didn't amount to anything at all."

First they flayed and cut up the cow. Then

they built a fireplace and placed a large flat rock over it to roast meat on. The fire soon flared up and the smoke drove away the intrusive mosquitoes. They wolfed down the grilled morsels and felt properly satisfied. The dream of the joys of the hunting life had come true.

They walked on and approached the hunting ground for reindeer bulls. It wasn't long before they spotted them–wonderful animals with towering antlers. They grazed while, from time to time, raising their heads to scent the air. Truly this was game worth hunting, the boys thought. They were gripped by a hunting lust they had not known before.

But they instinctively felt that they would have to carefully obey their father's instructions. Reindeer bulls could not be compared to suckling calves. They could also see from their father's expression that the hunt was to be pursued according to a different tactic.

They sneaked forward carefully, the boys right behind their father, watchful of his movements. When their father took aim, the boys did the same. Their father sought out an animal for himself and told the boys that, together, they should deal with another animal, which stood a little closer. The boys saw no reason to protest.

The shots rang out almost simultaneously. The bull that Tuumarsi had sought fell forwards and stayed down. The other bull leapt up while sand and small stones whipped up around it. Then it fell to the ground, as if its legs had given way beneath it, but a moment later it dashed off screaming. As it took a run attempting to leap over a rock, a sharp crack was heard and the bull fell forwards with its forelegs on the stone. Other animals had long ago taken flight, but since they apparently still were not acquainted with the danger of gunshot's, it wasn't long before they calmed down once more.

The boys were ecstatic with joy. When they reached the downed bulls, they grabbed ahold of the animal's antlers and felt the place on its back where the tallow had formed a hard mass.

Before evening they had shot another couple of bulls. Tuumarsi gave up on going further inland, as there were apparently enough reindeer where they were now. One also had to consider that all the prey had to be transported down to the camp at the coast. It is wonderful to hunt, but hard work carrying the prey.

17.

Each time Tuumarsi reached a reindeer hunting ground where other hunters had been and saw the remains of downed animals, yes indeed, sometimes entire carcasses, he would shake his head and wonder why the hunters then shot those animals, which they didn't really need. The only possible result this could have would be a reduction of the population.

He knew, from experience, of how the hunting zeal could develop into the desire for the senseless gunning down of animals. He could sense in the boys that they were eager to continue the hunt. But Tuumarsi said stop. It might be that they'd be able to supplement their hunting prey closer to the camp on the way home. And they could furthermore make one day trips out of the camp.

"When, sooner or later," he said to the boys, "you reach a place where hunters have been, you will discover that there are almost whole bodies of downed animals. Why must we down more than we can transport? In a few years it'll turn out that there'll be almost no reindeer to be found. In my early childhood we didn't have to go quite so far inland before we had found enough. Now that guns have become normal, we might expect the reindeer to be scared away."

The boys couldn't really understand this. Could there truly be any immediate danger of there not being enough reindeer, considering their volumes? Yet it was probably true, seeing as their father had said it.

They made their way home with their more or less bulky burdens on their backs. As they began to ache and the carrying straps cut into foreheads, the boys had to admit that it was easier to hunt than it was to carry the prey. After a while the youngest of the boys threw his burden onto the ground and shouted to his father that he should take some of the burden.

"Oh, and you even said that you'd not got enough reindeer. What would you have done if there had been more? We must each carry our own prey. If you can't carry what you're carrying right now, then you're not mature enough to take part in a reindeer hunt."

That threat had a revitalizing effect. Iisaaq bravely pulled himself together tremendously, shouldered his burden once more and followed the others.

During the arduous journey the boys suddenly heard their father shout: "People ahead." They quickly threw their burdens on the ground and looked around. Yes, there really were three people heading towards them.

The first thought the boys had was that they must be qivittut, fell walkers. They ran to their father, who had also put his burden down and had already gone to meet the strangers.

It turned out to be old acquaintances, people from Kangerluarsuk, father and son, Jensersuaq and Piitaq and their settlement-mate Hanseralak. It was a festive thing to meet so far inland.

Of course they began by talking about the reindeer hunt. The people from Kangerluarsuk said that they'd actually had a sufficient catch, but that they wanted to supplement their prey with some bulls.

"We took care of the bulls first. I thought the boys should experience a bull hunt. When we finish bringing our prey to the camp, we'll probably make another couple trips," said Tuumarsi and smiled to his boys.

"There were quite a few bulls where we were. But there were enough of the smaller animals as well," Jensersuaq countered.

"You'll get plenty of bulls when you get further inland," Tuumarsi said, finally.

They took advantage of the rest to fry some

reindeer steaks on a flat rock. When they had finished eating, they bid each other goodbye and went their separate ways.

In the afternoon of the following day, the reindeer hunters stood on a ridge some distance from the camp and announced their arrival with a couple of shots. Women and children rushed out of the tents and, shouting, came to meet them and help carry the heavy burdens the final stretch, much to the annoyance of Timuutu and Iisaaq, who had otherwise looked forward to demonstrating their skill in carrying the burdens. They had to put up with being hugged, praised and flattered. There they stood, smiling, and couldn't get a single word out. They had otherwise been looking forward to speaking about their hunting experiences.

In the camp, the smoke rose from the cooking sites, and there was a wonderful smell of cooked reindeer meat. The children ate tallow to the point where their faces and hands glistened with fat. Nobody stayed in the tents–everyone enjoying the good weather out in the open air. The sound of ulus being sharpened could be heard from time to time. Timuutu and Iisaaq told their peers about their experiences of reindeer hunting, but they started to stutter when they realized that the grown-ups were also listening to their account.

To feel like a hunter and know that the meat you are chewing was from one of your own catches was a wonderful sensation. In their own minds the boys stature grew large and they imagined being capable of stepping into their father's role as provider. Their father really ought to take things easy. They would do the catching and hunting so their mother would have something to put in the pots.

Yes, summer days, youthful days, days with prosperity and a life without worries!

Part Two

I.

In late autumn the Tuumarsi family returned to Naqerloq from their summer site. They had transported the majority of their winter supplies in advance, and now they returned with the last load. The summer trips were over.

They had been traveling all through the summer and the autumn. Ammassat catching, salmon fishing and reindeer hunting had followed right after one another. Seals, however, had no fixed season; they were hunted all year round. When the family finished stashing away their winter stores they thought: that is more than enough for winter consumption.

More people had come to Naqerloq. Those who did less well during the last winter and had decided to move came back in the autumn with more people in their wake. Andariarsi the reader started his lessons with some tenacity and had for some reason begun to act with greater firmness towards his pupils. But this tenacity would probably wane as the winter progressed.

When the men gathered at their usual gathering spot this autumn, completely new subjects were discussed and spoken of. Piitrusi had been at the colony site for almost the entire summer and had been a rower in the priest's boat on a trip to Holsteinsborg. Many found what he had experienced there to be exciting, and he scrounged himself many a cup of coffee and plug of tobacco for his long pipe, which he had been gifted by a Danish benefactor. He had also obtained a cap, of which he was very proud, he even kept it on his head when he was out rowing in his kayak.

As far as experiences were concerned, he was in competition with Joorsuaat, the readers son-in-law. He also had something to say about things which were at least as exciting. He had been to Godthåb (Nuuk) as a rower in the colony manager's boat. You should have seen the church, there was no other house so big. Yes, when speaking of big houses, then one couldn't forget the houses of the priest and the inspector. And the inspector himself! What clothes he wore. He had golden things on his coat and on his hat, and they shone in the sun to the point where your eyes hurt to look at them. Then Joorsuaat would laugh and preen himself, for he was the only one in Naqerloq who had experienced such things. Andariarsi's reply was the usual: "And here we are without even a lousy shop!" Andariarsi received a fixed salary as a reader. It was paid out to him by the catechist in Ikerasassuaq, when the latter came to Naqerloq to inspect things. If there was a shop there, then Andariarsi could impress the others, who did not have money, by taking the carefully folded shopping list out of his pocket and listing all the things he wanted to buy! And when the money had run out, well, then there was probably the possibility of getting things on credit—for he was a reader on a fixed salary!

Giitioorsuaq had also come reindeer hunting. He was probably the most experienced reindeer hunter in Naqerloq, but each time he began to speak of his experiences on the reindeer hunts, people walked away, led by Piitrusi and Joorsuaat, who had far more exciting things to recount. Giitioorsuaq was not one to be perturbed by the lack of an audience. He babbled on, some times without an audience, and other times he only had his son Aggu, Tuumarsi and a couple of oldsters as an audience.

In such a gathering Tuumarsi would be practically silent. He was sorry that people had arrived that preferred to live carelessly. He knew that both Piitrusi and Joorsuaat and their families hadn't collected enough winter supplies. Now they walked around without thinking of the winter, preening themselves over their summer adventures. Tuumarsi couldn't help but compare himself with such people. He had heard several times his own household comment to him that surely there must now be enough winter supplies. His answer was always the same: "That which seems enough during the summer often turns out not to suffice during the winter. It is more greedy than the summer." His wife hinted, now and then, that she would like to revisit the colony site, to which Tuumarsi laughingly replied: "You can do that when I am gone."

Tuumarsi knew that the newcomers were in opposition to those who had founded the site, and accused them of taking too dominant a position. But he accepted this as fact. Time would show who was right.

2.

Tuumarsi's mother had been ailing for a long time and she had often been bedridden. At the start of the winter she remained there, and she knew that she wouldn't get up again. Her family also realized where things were headed.

Suffering coughs, shortness of breath and chest pains, she often thought of her life so far. So much had happened! The little girl that had been born and raised far, far to the north, had, in a remarkable way, left her original home and had had children and grandchildren. And now she was the oldest person in the settlement. People's evil towards one another had chased the little innocent girl from her home, and maybe she was to leave this world in the knowledge that discord still existed among people. There were examples of this, even in a little place like Naqerloq.

When she thought about her life, her thoughts mainly focused on the only child she'd had that was still alive, Tuumarsi.

Tuumarsi had grown up in love and care at his parents side. He had not been a happy boy. He had not partaken much in the games of other children. He had mostly preferred to stay at home and keep to himself. When he was out, he preferred to be present among the men and listen to their tales of catching and hunting. As a mother she had not been unfamiliar with the boy, in a more mature age, not always being at peace at home. It was as if he couldn't thrive in the atmosphere created by his father's religious stance. This could be felt in his reactions to his father's predictions. His parents had sometimes spoken of it, but they had not let on about this to their son. But beyond that he had behaved as a good son, who clearly didn't want to cause his parents grief.

After his father's death, Tuumarsi suddenly became a grown man. He was definitely a son that a mother could be proud of. She had often wished that his father could have seen this development, so they could have delighted in it together.

Tuumarsi was in many ways different than his father. He was more manly, more self-aware and diligent. He must obviously have thought that his father's lack of diligence in his profession as a hunter must have been caused by his monotonously Christian attitude, and he must have had the perception that a Christian attitude and full devotion to the hunting profession simply couldn't mesh. Tuumarsi had chosen the latter. But things had since changed. The Christian attitude and the hunter's profession had grown to supplement each other in him in an excellent way, and created a firm bulwark against destructive forces from outside.

When the old woman reached this point in her reflections, she felt as if she was being lifted up into higher altitudes, and as if she gained a clearer understanding of her problems. But when she woke and felt the pain in her breath and was plagued by shortness of breath, then she knew that she was an old, sick woman, who couldn't even raise a hand to help out with the women's work in the home. She let her eyes wander around the house. She spoke about doing this and that, but her speech descended into pure nonsense, while the grandchildren gazed at her dumbstruck.

3.

One evening, when the others had gone to rest, and while the night-light emitted its weak light, Tuumarsi sat with his chest bare on the edge of the benches and looked at his mother, who lay mumbling something in a partial stupor while pictures from the past passed before his eyes.

He thought of his parents, and he once more felt guilty for the lack of esteem he had had for them in his childhood. But this evening he was calmer in the knowledge that he had been forgiven for this.

With a start, his mother awoke.

"Tuumarsi," she whispered.

"Yes, do you want some water?" he whispered back.

"I have dreamt. I have had a strange dream, Tuumarsi, are you awake?"

"Yes, I've not gone to bed yet. Sleep does you good. You're not even coughing."

"I have dreamt. Are the others awake?"

"No, they are all asleep."

"Listen to me, Tuumarsi. You must not be afraid. Everything proceeds according to God's will. But alas, why on earth did we have descendants? What fate can they expect? I am worried about them. Tuumarsi, I have always trusted you. You have always been a good son to your father and me. Keep being good and things will probably go better."

Tears came to Tuumarsi's eyes, but since he thought his mother was speaking in a delirium, he softly said: "Try to go to sleep now, mother. Or should I perhaps wake Kaluliit?"

"No, don't do that. Can I tell you my dream?"

"Yes, I can hear you, even if you whisper."

"Before I fell asleep, I happened to think of a tale that you once told the children, the one about a young man called Juuserfi. It was something about him interpreting the dream of a king. I don't know why I happened to think about that. After I fell asleep, I dreamt that I sat at a big river, and that I was wearing very fine clothes. Then I spotted some animals—they looked like reindeer, but they had short horns—and they climbed out of the river. They were fat, so fat that they could barely walk. When they vanished from sight, I saw more of the same type, just as many of the first, and they also climbed out of the river. But they were so gaunt, so gaunt, that the bones almost broke through their skin. They went up to the first ones and ate them, but you couldn't tell from looking at them, because their bellies were as thin as before."

Then she paused, tired of speaking. She

breathed heavily. Tuumarsi sat and listened tensely without saying anything. He sweated to the point that water ran down his face, but still he trembled with the cold.

"Are you listening?" his mother asked.

"Yes," he mumbled.

"Then I saw a man in splendid clothing, surrounded by emaciated people who lifted their arms up towards him. I saw that they moved their lips, but I didn't hear what they said. The man carried a big sack, and from it he poured something that looked like flour, and he gave it to the people that stood around him. When he wanted to hand something to a very gaunt and frightened looking man, the giver raised his face. And it was your face I saw, Tuumarsi, and the way he did it reminded me a lot of yours, when you give your youngest something to eat. The man that he handed something to, fell to his knees, and I saw that it was one of our fellow residents."

Then she paused again and breathed heavily, almost rattling. Tuumarsi felt as if ice cold water was being poured down his back, and his entire body was shaking. He could hear his heart beating, and he could neither get up, nor speak.

"Are you listening?" his mother whispered. "Are you listening?"

Tuumarsi would rather have screamed, had he been able, and tell his mother to stop talking. But with the greatest of efforts he moved his lips and managed to mumble a "yes."

"After a while I noticed," his mother continued, "that I was alone. Everything was quiet around me. Then I saw a big and splendid house, and I made my way there. It was so scary! Dead people lay side-by-side in all the passages and rooms. In the end I went into a small room, and there, alone on the benches, lay the man with the splendid clothes. I could barely recognize him. He had grown so gaunt, and his hair and beard had grown. As I placed myself beside him, he turned his eyes towards me and smiled. He took my hand and placed it upon his chest, and while I looked at him, he closed his eyes and moved no more. In that exact moment, I felt his hand go limp and I awakened."

She turned her eyes to her son and asked: "Are you listening?"

Tuumarsi didn't reply. Just after he had muttered his last "yes," he had felt as if he was sinking into the great nothingness and had lost consciousness. He hadn't managed to hear the last part of his mother's tale.

Tuumarsi regained consciousness with his wife shaking him, and he heard the children crying. Shaking with the cold, he hurriedly crept under the blanket, and he fell asleep at once.

4.

Tuumarsi's mother died a couple of days later. It was early in the morning, with the entire household and part of Giitioorsuaq's household gathered around her. Tuumarsi, who had been ill since the evening when he heard his mother's account, and who had only just now recovered, placed his mother's folded hands on her chest.

The weeping of women and children could be heard. With tears in his eyes, Tuumarsi led his children to their grandmother one by one, so that they could see her one last time. Calm and collected, he looked at his mother, who had peacefully passed away in her sleep. Since the night where she had told him of her dream, she had been almost completely unconscious, and she had been completely calm when she woke.

A psalm was sung. Tuumarsi tried to join in, but, overcome by emotion, he had to give up.

People came in and left again. Everyone wanted to say goodbye to this lovable woman, the oldest of the settlement. People came and went all through the morning. Only Giitioorsuaq stayed. Without a word he sat, as if guarding the deceased, who was now gone and now left him, Giitioorsuaq, with the position of being the oldest at the site. From time to time he would wipe away his tears with the end of his sleeve.

In the afternoon, people were ready to place the deceased in a body-skin. Tuumarsi decided that the very best depilated sealskin they had in the house was to be used. Nobody said a word while the skins were sown together around the body, only the sound of the needle penetrating the skin and a faint sobbing could be heard.

Tuumarsi asked the reader to read the lord's prayer, and Andariarsi did so with a trembling voice. His amen was repeated by Tuumarsi and Giitioorsuaq.

Following a psalm, the body was carried out to the side room in the entrance passage. Tuumarsi hung skins up in front of the entrance and placed stones at the bottom so nobody could get in.

Three days later a funeral was held. The weather was good, but nobody went hunting. Dressed in their best clothes, people gathered at noon at Tuumarsi's place, as many as space allowed. Many had to stay outside.

In the middle of the floor, the body lay wrapped in skins. After a psalm, the reader Andariarsi spoke of the scriptures tale of old Simeon, who in his old age had waited for the Savior's arrival and the peace he felt having seen him. Andariarsi sweated so much that the water ran down his face. In a way this was all part of a good speech.

Afterwards people walked to the burial site. The deceased was placed in the grave and Andariarsi threw the earth onto the body: "From earth have you come, to earth you will become, and from the earth you will resurrect. Amen."

"Amen," said Tuumarsi, with a trembling voice.

"Amen," finished Giitioorsuaq, simultaneously throwing back his anorak hood.

5.

In the following years the weather and hunting conditions were good in Naqerloq, even during the winter. Tuumarsi had good reason to be satisfied, as he, a provider, received good help from his sons. Timuutu had grown to become a skilled hunter, full of energy and enthusiasm for his task. Tuumarsi could not help but think of his own situation at that age, and for the most part let him do what he wanted, provided he obeyed his advice and instructions. The second oldest, Iisaaq, had also come along well. He did well at kayaking and had already caught quite a few seals. But his father still wouldn't let him go hunting alone in his kayak. He was only allowed to go out along with him, or his uncle. When Iisaaq wasn't allowed to go hunting on the open sea, he went bird hunting nearby along with his peers.

Timuutu and Iisaaq had, right from their first practice in rowing kayaks, learned how to turn around in them. They recalled, with amusement, how exciting it was when their father had to teach them this art. Wearing full-furs (see glossary), they had gone down to the beach, got into their kayaks, pulled the face-opening of the full-fur tight, and grabbed their kayak oars in the way that they should, held their breath and waited for their father, who held onto the front tip of the kayak, to turn it around. To begin with, when they went under water, they were so frightened that they couldn't figure out the elementary practices of moving the oars in a certain way to get up. And when their father had helped them and been amused by their breathlessness, he repeated his instructions. The boys were ready to try again to impress their friends, who watched the exercises with great amusement.

In the end they had learned how to turn around with the help of the kayak oar. They had also learned how to hold their breath for longer and longer under water as the exercises gradually took place in deeper water.

And the exercises continued. Timuutu was, as the eldest, the most advanced, and he was now also able to turn with the help of his lance and throwing wood. These exercises had been of use to him in several instances. He had, at one point, the misfortune of being dragged down by a harpooned seal, causing him to capsize. This was out in the open sea. But before the others could reach him, he had righted himself unaided. It was things like this that filled his father with pride and joy. And not only that, but Timuutu had on several occasions shown himself capable of handling troubled seas, indeed even stormy seas.

Tuumarsi therefore had good reason to feel joy in the boys' growth and development as providers. And it was understandable that he was optimistic about the future and felt at ease.

6.

One morning, as they woke, they took a look at the weather before leaving, as always, and this morning they did so even more thoroughly than usual. It was dead calm, but there was a weak and warm air from the south. They felt they could probably go out, since the clouds weren't moving much. It was also mentioned that Giitioorsuaq didn't have any pains in his knee. He usually felt changes in the weather because of the arthritis he suffered from. It ended with the hunters leaving somewhat later than they usually would.

Tuumarsi was of two minds. He would gladly go, but he didn't like the weak, warm air that came from the south. He tried to convince Timuutu to stay at home, but let him go anyway when his uncle said that he would accompany him. Perhaps he shouldn't have given in, but on the other hand there was no reason to keep young people that were keen to hunt at home without any particular reason. In addition he trusted Timuutu's skills as a kayak-rower and felt that he was in good hands with the other, more experienced, kayak-rowers.

Throughout the morning and a good part of the afternoon he was purely occupied by looking at the weather. By the time the hunters would probably have reached the furthest hunting areas, the first clouds appeared on the eastern horizon, and clouds formed around the top of the great fell. Then Tuumarsi was certain: A tempest was in the offing, a south easterly with snow. He was gripped by turmoil, and he bitterly regretted having given Timuutu permission to go. He hoped they were sensible enough to make their way home the moment they suspected something.

Some men stood at the kayak frames, hunting veterans, knowledgeable weather prophets. He went over to them. They stood with their hands in their trouser pockets, looking at the weather and speaking worriedly about the hunters that had gone out. When Tuumarsi came over to them they were almost aghast.

"Eh, eh, have you stayed home?"

"I am very troubled. Nobody should have left in such weather. Has everyone gone?"

Giitioorsuaq had also come, in spite of the arthritic pains in his knee. He replied that almost everyone had gone. Only two kayaks lay on the western frame.

"I should not have given Timuutu permission to go," Tuumarsi said, "I only gave him permission because his uncle went. But what about your youths?"

"It is impossible to keep the young ones at home," Giitioorsuaq replied. "Aggu left without my knowledge. Had he asked he wouldn't have been given permission—it doesn't look too good. One can only hope that they are on their way home. Is there nobody who can go to warn them?"

It was clear that they were all very troubled. And their disquiet had not been lessened by finding out that Tuumarsi had stayed at home. They knew that he only stayed at home when he truly had a reason to. But as they stood there, some bare headed boys arrived, kicking a ball.

"Where is your reader?"

"He has gone."

"Is there really nobody that can go out to see to them?" Giitioorsuaq sad, "if only I were..."

"I will go," said Tuumarsi. "If nothing else I can try to help them find shelter."

7.

The kayakers that had left in the morning accompanied each other to the hunting area. They were eager to hunt, and the weather didn't worry them. They separated there. Timuutu and his uncle were located furthest to the west.

They had made a good start at searching the area for seals when they noticed that clouds were forming in an alarming way. They simultaneously also noticed an increasing breeze from the south east.

Timuutu and his uncle suspected something and decided to row inland. But it didn't seem that the other hunters were going to do the same. When the seals began to pop up, they gave up on their plan and focused on the hunt.

Timuutu had caught a seal and started to prepare it to be towed when they saw that the other kayaks were turning their noses homewards. The uncle hurried his nephew, as the sea could quickly become tumultuous. When the other kayakers signaled with their arms for them to join them, they also began to row inwards, Timuutu with his seal in tow. The wind grew stronger and stronger, and it began to snow. The kayakers stayed close to one another so as not to lose sight of anyone. The most experienced kayak-rower, Aalibak, led the way. He headed for an island where the best options for getting ashore were. They had the wind behind them and managed a good speed, but the distance to the island was great.

Suddenly the storm arrived, and it brought heavy snow with it. The sea and the sky became as one, and the hunters had a hard time seeing and contacting each other. They shouted and screamed to avoid losing each other and tried to keep to the direction indicated by their leader.

"Cut your catch loose, we need more speed," the uncle shouted to Timuutu.

It only took a moment for Timuutu to free himself from his catch, and he didn't care about the loss. It was now all about finding shelter ashore as quickly as possible. They were careful not to lose sight of one another.

"Look out, look out," the uncle shouted. Timuutu only just managed to prepare to accept the wave. They were buried in the heaving water and held their breath. Slowly the kayaks came to the surface again.

"Do let me know if you can't manage any more," the uncle shouted, "then I'll support you." The uncle couldn't help but feel a certain pride in the fact that his nephew could handle such violent breakers. "When we get near the others, avoid winding up on their leeward side. You risk them being thrown against you by the waves. Instead, stick to my leeward side."

They couldn't see the others any more, and they couldn't hear anyone shout. It was simply a matter of sticking to the assumed direction. The uncle had enough to take care of, but he still couldn't help but think of the young kayak-rowers that had come on this trip. Even he had never experienced being out in such a violently troubled sea as this.

The storm and the snowfall grew even more violent. One breaker after another broke over them. Will we make it? Will we make it? This was the constantly recurring thought. Yes, they managed this time. Slowly they emerged from the water masses. The uncle insisted on supporting his nephew to prevent capsizing, but Timuutu preferred to try and take care of himself—for as long as he could.

They rowed on. When the breakers came in faster and faster one after another, they knew that they were near shore. They were right. Through the falling snow they discovered a cliff face against which the breakers beat with massive force.

"That won't work," the uncle shouted, "we can't get ashore there. Row backwards as best you can until we can turn. Perhaps we can find an inlet once we've gotten around the headland."

Making a turn was hard work, as the front end of the kayak was constantly turned back by the force of the wind. They had to row hard against it and the waves to avoid being thrown against the cliff. They had to, and needed to, get further out before they could turn and get around the headland. Timuutu rowed with all his might, but he felt that he was growing tired, and that his strength was no match for this fight against the elements. He would rather turn around right away.

"I can't do this any more," he shouted to his uncle, who was a little ahead of him. "Lets turn around, it doesn't matter where we land."

"Then we'll do that," his uncle shouted back, "But stay as close to the wind as possible."

As they turned, they discovered something dark directly ahead of them. It was a capsized kayak. A depressing sight for those fighting for their lives. Should they perhaps try to save him? The thought occurred to Timuutu.

"Stay away from it," the uncle shouted, having guessed Timuutu's thoughts. "We can't carry out a rescue attempt in weather like this." Timuutu barely managed to avoid having the kayak land on him.

They managed to round the southern point of the headland and carefully turn so that they got the wind at their backs. The beach ahead was white with the foam of the waves, and the beating of the breakers against the cliffs almost drowned out the noise of the storm. Then they spotted some men who stood a good distance from the shore and waved them in. It seemed there were some that had managed to save themselves—and who were ready to help others, but it was too dangerous for them to go all the way down to the shore.

"When the next wave breaks, ride it and do your best to be thrown ashore. You must be ready to get out of the kayak, and if you can't pull it further up the beach, then leave it be. Be ready, here comes the wave. Hold tight to your oar."

Timuutu rode the wave and had a good turn of speed. He heard a shout from the men on land, pushed the kayak-oar under the cross-strap in front of him and tried to get out. But he hadn't time to loosen the kayak fur, which was tied to the kayak ring, and while he was in the process of loosening it, he realized that he was moving backwards. As he felt his kayak fill with water, he tried to grab his oar, but it was gone. After a moment's confusion he managed to twist his way out of the kayak and tried to cling to it.

The uncle couldn't see anything, and he thought that his nephew had managed to get ashore. He rode the next wave and was thrown up onto the beach where he barely managed to free himself from his kayak before he was pulled ashore. The wave took the kayak back with it.

Warned by the shouts, he turned around and looked outwards. His nephew lay out there thrown back and forth by the waves, and his kayak was a good distance from him. Judging by his movements one could see that he was trying to reach shore, but it was as if the waves were using him as a ball. Sobbing, the uncle went back and forth trying to find something with which to save his nephew, and when he, in his despair, grabbed the only saved kayak, the other had to stop in his hopeless endeavor. There was no reason for more people to lose their lives. He turned his face away so as not to see more.

He turned around at the sound of some shouts, and he looked outwards again. A kayaker had come into sight, who seemed to investigate the possibilities for landing. Without thinking of the dangerous situation the kayaker was in, Timuutu's uncle shouted out to him and used his arms to direct his attention to the victim. It was uncertain if the kayaker had noticed it, but he certainly turned suddenly and rowed over towards a dark object which appeared from the waves one moment and vanished the next. If this kayaker was really attempting a rescue, then he had to be an unusually good kayak-rower. The men ashore looked on with unbearable tension and followed everything that happened. The kayaker reached the victim and, in a trice, attached his harpoon strap to his arm. Then he picked a breaker to ride and headed ashore with good speed. The onlookers were speechless with dismay—who did not know this kayaker, it was Tuumarsi—towing his son's body with no idea who it was. The uncle fainted and fell over in the snow.

Tuumarsi quickly got out of the kayak and pulled both it and the victim onto the beach. Shortly after, the father carried his dead son ashore.

8.

Tuumarsi could never understand, later, how he—having discovered that the victim was his own son—had had the strength to carry him ashore. He must have done it almost without realizing. Only when he had placed his son in a place where the waves couldn't reach, had he come to his senses and laid himself on top of him, as if he thought he could, through his own body heat, bring him back to life. He had forgotten everything around him. It had been as if everything had gone quiet, and all had been shrouded in darkness. His thoughts had centered on only one thing: Timuutu. Timuutu, are you asleep, or are you dead? To begin with he had shaken his son to wake him up. Then he had lost consciousness and laid down without moving.

The others sat close against each other to stay warm and looked at father and son, immovable together.

After much time had passed, Tuumarsi slowly got up. He took his full-fur off and placed it upon his son's face and chest. The tears had frozen to his cheeks, and pieces of ice clung to his moustache. He went over to the knot of men that sat together and asked them, with a weak voice, how they were.

The storm had finally abated, and the snowfall was almost over. The sky was clearing.

"I am going back now. You will be taken back by an umiak, just as soon as the weather improves. Make sure to keep warm. Keep an eye on him—he pointed at his son—not because there is anything that can be done. The weather has been too rough for a young man like that."

With slow steps he walked towards his kayak. When he was unable to carry his kayak alone, one of the men had to help him, and—after Tuumarsi had got into the kayak—push it away from shore. After a while he rounded the headland and was lost from sight.

When Tuumarsi was alone it first truly struck him how hard it hit him to lose his son. His hopes for the future now lay in pieces. But the worst thing for him was to think that a young, happy man, who had been a joy to all in the home, was no longer among the living. What was he to say when he returned? It would be a heavy and sad message to bring to Timuutu's mother and siblings.

Just before he rounded the Naqerloq headland he wiped his tears away for the last time. As was customary when arriving with news of an accident, he headed towards the beach with long pauses between oar strokes and with his head bowed. His fellow residents, who had come down to receive him, understood the message he brought. But how many? Who? Such tension!

Tuumarsi let himself be pulled up onto the beach, still with his head bowed. Nobody asked, all were silent. Among the few women that turned up, sobbing and sniffing could be heard, and several men had tears in their eyes.

Tuumarsi straightened himself up: "Paaluseeraq, Ujuaansi and Janna stayed out there.

Timuutu's body was brought ashore—the others are safe. Buaasi, please go tell Kaluliit, gently, that Timuutu . . ." and then he could manage no more.

It was a day of sorrow and despair in Naqerloq.

9.

In the time following, life was sad in Naqerloq. Two hunters, who were both sole providers, and two promising young men had lost their lives, and this left its mark on the daily life. And not only that, but one of those that were saved, Joorsuaat, had received internal injuries during the rescue attempts, and he died after a protracted illness.

The disaster struck hardest on those that had become widows or orphans. Paaluseeraq and Janna had been sole providers for two houses, and their passing was a heavy blow to those left behind. But their fellow residents set on ensuring that the didn't want for necessities, so long as they could be obtained. Not just because it was an unwritten law in a hunting community, but also because the disaster felt shared by all.

Tuumarsi had had a hard time adjusting to what had happened. He almost lived in a dream world. He couldn't even express his sorrow. Only when the umiak, which rescued the survivors from their refuge, returned, and he witnessed for himself how the survivors either walked unaided or were helped up to the houses, while his son's frozen corpse was carried up to his house, did he wake to reality. Timuutu had come home, but as a frozen corpse, and he had been placed in the side room of the entrance corridor. The smaller siblings had been told that Timuutu had come, and that he was now in the side room. They constantly asked when he would come in, and they wanted to go out to see him. Tuumarsi couldn't bear this. He decided that the burial would take place as soon as possible. So Timuutu was buried the day after his return home.

The foaming waves on the sea outside Naqerloq bore witness to the funeral. The mourners could not keep back their tears, for the funeral was simultaneously a remembrance ceremony for those men the sea had taken. After the grave had been covered, everyone went their separate ways. Nobody was out catching, everyone was at home and silently sitting with bowed heads, thinking of the men that had, over time, been taken by the sea.

For the first while after the disaster, the hunters stayed home. It was as if they were afraid of the great sea, which had revealed its strength and had reminded these small people that it was futile to defy its power.

But they lived in a small, isolated hunting community, and their existence depended upon the sea. People couldn't stay home and allow the sea to dictate hunting conditions. Food had to be brought in. One couldn't simply rely on winter stores alone. The population of Naqerloq had experienced kayak accidents several times before, but they had never witnessed this many perishing at once; they had never thought that such things could happen.

10.

Something now happened which Tuumarsi and his family had feared. He had to surrender to his outer and inner sufferings. It was clear that a heart condition, which had tormented him before, had grown worse.

Tuumarsi didn't take it all that seriously, however, as he felt that it would pass of its own accord. His inner suffering was worse though. His thoughts always centered upon his dead son, and he saw him from dawn to dusk, day and night. If only he had looked as he had when he was alive, then it might not have been so bad. But to see him as a frozen corpse was more than Tuumarsi could bear.

It was difficult for a father, who throughout the best part of his manhood had sought to ensure the continuation of his family, to be given a blow which suddenly destroyed these efforts and hopes. He couldn't manage to start over again. It was as if he pushed the thought of raising his others sons away from him.

He no longer thought about what the reason and meaning of this tragedy might be, for it had to be God that let it happen. The God that rules over humans, and who can cut the thread of life when he sees fit. When despair overwhelmed him, he had a great desire to curse God. But it had never quite got to that point.

He remained in this condition for several days, sleepless and tormented by his thoughts. He had gradually grown so confused that his sorrow had slipped into the background. It was as if he realized what was actually wrong with him. He called upon God and asked that he preserve his senses and prevent him from doing anything drastic: "Lead me not into temptation, but deliver me from evil."

He had become very gaunt: he didn't eat, nor have any appetite. His wife, Kaluliit, had also been struck by sorrow's paralyzing blow. On being informed of her son's demise, she had fallen over in a faint and since then had trouble overcoming his sorrow. But now she had pulled herself together. There was a lot of work needing to be done in the house, and she had to look after and take care of her husband. She first and foremost had to prevent him going "mad." She did this by trying to get him to eat something and getting him to sleep. She spoke to him of things that might divert his thoughts.

One evening Tuumarsi sat in his usual place in the house and fell asleep. Then, suddenly, he nodded his head and was, in a trice, wide awake. The same thing happened several times, and in the end he fell into a deep sleep.

"To think, he has fallen asleep," Kaluliit thought, astonished. She would have liked him to lay down on the benches, but she dared not touch him, lest she risk waking him. She carefully placed a pillow behind his head and told the children to be quiet. She sat down next to her husband, and she sat and cried in silence with happy anticipation of this being the start of his recovery.

This proved to be the case. The next day, late in the morning, Tuumarsi woke and asked for something to eat. Then he burst into tears, for the first time since the death of his son. It was a liberating grief. The others in the house couldn't keep back their grief.

It felt as if the grief had chased away the dark that had lain over Tuumarsi, without and within. A clearing had come. The thoughts that wandered in great confusion had once more settled on their proper courses and calmed down. Why have I only occupied myself with my own grief and not thought of the others, whose grief is greater than mine? Why should I not bear my misfortune when the others can? Have I not other sons that I can raise? When God, in his wisdom, has robbed others of their dear ones, why should he make an exception for me?

Tuumarsi thanked God for having liberated him from his sickness, and he asked for forgiveness if he had, in his thoughts and actions, done something that was unseemly in God's eyes. He thanked his Gods for not having treated him differently from the others. Now he felt even more obliged to help those left behind by those that had perished, as a poor offering of thanks.

He simultaneously wished that there be a memento of the incident that taught him God's power, justice and wisdom. So he wrote to the catechist in Ikerasassuaq and asked him to make a plaque, which he could hang on the wall. It was to read:

"The Lord gave, the Lord took, the Lord's name be praised!"

II.

The winter had brought disaster and now the sorrow was over. The summer sun and the summer activities had chased the sorrow away. News of the disaster had long ago reached far and wide, and in all places it made a deep impression. Wherever the population of Naqerloq went on their spring journey, they were greeted with signs of sympathy. But this simply causes the wounds from the sorrow to bleed again, the sorrow that they had tried to chase from their minds.

While Tuumarsi was in Ammassivik, the catechist from Ikerasassuaq came to perform a service. Immediately after arriving he visited Tuumarsi's family in their tent. He had a small, square package with him. He unwrapped it and passed it to Tuumarsi.

It was a piece of paper, glued to cardboard, framed with black-painted wood. Written with neat letters, and with a cross underneath, stood:

Nalekkap tunniukkamiok
Nalekkap tigova
Nalekkap arka kujanarsilæt

Tuumarsi looked at what had been written for a long time, in silence. He knew what it said, but from the movement of his lips one could tell that he was re-reading it again and again. Finally he opened up his little chest and placed the memorial plaque inside.

While Tuumarsi crept his way through the text, the catechist observed him and noticed that he had become much older. He didn't look like the man that, when he moved to Naqerloq, had an upright figure with plump cheeks and jet-black hair, cut at the brow. A young man who could be glib and well-spoken, with a sharp laughter. An agile man and an eager participant of tests of strength. Now the same man sat hunched, with a wrinkled face and tufts of beard here and there. His unruly hair was speckled with grey, his facial expression mild, but without a hint of a smile. Only the sinewy hands showed that he was still a strong man. He looked as if he had lost interest in what went on around him. The aging catechist suddenly felt younger than Tuumarsi.

The inhabitants of the tent left, so the catechist and Tuumarsi were alone.

"You experienced a great sorrow over the winter. The ways of the lord are inscrutable," the catechist began.

"Yes, it was especially difficult to begin with," Tuumarsi said. "I never thought that a sorrow could be so hard to bear. Thankfully it is now over, so to speak."

"We have felt with you in your sorrow. And

we also share your thankfulness for it now being over."

"It was a time where I felt completely knocked out, and didn't have the ability to recover from it. The after-effects have probably left their marks on my exterior, on my body and on my face, but I can now say that I am completely well inside. You are a catechist and at the same time also a good acquaintance, for which reason I feel an urge to tell you something I have not entrusted to anyone else. It began with me convincing myself that I was the only one affected by the disaster. For the others, worse affected than me, I gave not a thought. When I realized that the man I brought ashore was my son, I didn't want to believe it. Only once he had been brought home and buried did the truth dawn on me. The sorrow over the death of our son, the son we had brought up to the best of our ability, and in whom we had placed our hopes, knocked me out so entirely that I couldn't even sleep. Things went downhill to the extent that I was afraid of losing my mind. Then I called upon our maker with all my soul to free me from my misery. One evening, when I was very low and felt as if my head was going to explode, I was suddenly overwhelmed by tiredness and fell asleep. Much later I woke up and realized that my senses had returned with full clarity, and that I had reattained the ability to think about things.

Why should I think only of myself? Several families had lost providers. I am still able to carry out my profession as a hunter, and I have sons that—if all goes well—I can train. My own situation is nothing compared to that of others. The Lord has been merciful on me. I should be ashamed of my own selfishness and lack of ability to understand the maker's vicissitudes. When the Lord in his great wisdom took the only providers from their families, why should he make an exception of me? After I had been able to make such calm considerations, I found peace, a peace that goes beyond comprehension. I then thanked the Lord for his mercy and compassion towards me. As poor thanks, I have promised myself to do my part to ensure that bereaved do not suffer want."

The catechist had listened to Tuumarsi's confession silently, and with bowed head. When he fell silent, the catechist stood up with tears in his eyes, offered his hand with a smile and said:

"Tuumarsi, we can all learn from what you have been through. You, more than any of us, have come to know the righteous ways of the Lord. Your faith is strong. I was right in my perception of you after all."

Then they spoke of various everyday things. It had been a good moment for both of them.

12.

Tuumarsi now began to seriously teach his son Iisaaq. He was the eldest of the children, and as such had to be raised with the continuation of the family in mind. He was now a skilled kayak rower and an industrious hunter. He was ambitious and fully aware of his duties as co-provider. But he often missed his brother, with whom he had performed exciting exercises, competitions, hunts and fishing trips.

After the accident, the number of people in Naqerloq had waned. Several families had moved to their relatives at other settlements. Now, seven years after the death of Tuumarsi's mother, there were only five houses with seven families. Of the original inhabitants, only Tuumarsi's and Aggu's families—Giitioorsuaq had died two years ago—Tuumarsi's brother-in-law and his family, and a couple of others remained as fixed residents. The reader Andariarsi and his family had also moved, and Aggu now acted as reader, thus following in the footsteps of his father.

They suffered no want. There was game enough for those few hunters. They had experienced good and bad together, and on the basis of their experiences, they could now organize their existence in fellowship and harmony. As usual they ensured that their storerooms were filled by the start of winter. Even if the ice were to place barriers in the way of hunting activity for a while, they would no doubt make it though the winter.

The young—the next generation—was raised and trained according to the advice and instructions of the elders. It was all about ensuring the continued existence of the family.

13.

Autumn came. Bad weather and an unpleasant, persistent westerly wind set in. The ice could be expected to drift in at any time. The hunters got very little out of their journeys, on the rare occasion that they could defy the weather and venture out.

The families in Naqerloq were forced to eat into their winter supplies. They did so reluctantly, but it was necessary. It was too early in the year, but there was nothing else to do. Meanwhile they hoped that the weather would change, and that the game animals would present themselves. That which they gained from their hunting trips, from time to time, couldn't even cover the needs of a single day.

One day, in the beginning of the Christmas month, a thin, white strip appeared on the horizon. This could only mean one thing: ice, which, as expected, approached. Slowly but surely.

In the following days the strip grew wider and wider. The hunters devoted every energy to scouring the sea for prey before it was closed off, but it was as if the sea had been swept clean of animals.

In the middle of the month, the ice reached all the way into Naqerloq, and before Christmas everything on the waters around the place was white. The settlement and its population was cut off from the outside world.

How futile it was! The hunters set off across

the packed ice, carrying their kayaks on their heads in order to find any openings. They did find open water at some of the (water current) sites, but there was no prey. They could fish there in a pinch, and sometimes caught a bit.

The winter supplies dwindled fast, and rationing became necessary. The result was that nobody had enough to eat. People began to wear away. The gaunt dogs had to be butchered and eaten.

One day three hunters left to try and reach the edge of the ice. They took their kayaks with them. On the third day, in the evening, they came home, completely weakened by their long stay on the ice in the cold weather. They had shot a fjord seal, but during their efforts to reach it they had fallen several times into the water between the ice floes, and had only managed to avoid freezing to death by digging themselves down under the snow. They only had a bit of the seal left, not even enough to provide a bite for everyone. That only made the hunger more palpable. They had had to leave one of the kayaks out there. The hunters time and time again tried heading off in all directions. Tuumarsi had been out on a two-day trip with his son Iisaaq, but had come home empty-handed, which was very disheartening for everyone. When even Tuumarsi failed, well, there was not much left to hope for.

14.

When the men were forced to stay home, they passed the time by standing at their usual meeting point. They stood there with their hands buried deeply in their trouser pockets, coughing, and with haggard faces. It was hard to believe that these were the same men that previously—an eternity ago—had stood, glad and satisfied, bristling with health. When the topic of conversation—weather and the bad hunting conditions, the same again and again—had been exhausted, they went home to their houses, where at least it was warmer than out in the cold. There was no heating in most of the houses; the warming oil lamps were not lit. The remaining stocks of blubber and oil were now only reserved for distribution in small portions as a supplement to dried meat and fish.

At Christmas someone came to beg food at Tuumarsi's house for the first time, and they didn't leave the house empty-handed. At Christmas nobody should want food. Later, when the distress was greatest with those who, in spite of the frugality, had run out of winter stores, Tuumarsi opened his storerooms. The modern day Joseph distributed food to his subjects.

Incidents were now related where people didn't have the strength to get out of bed. The lack of nourishing food sucked the resilience out of healthy and sick people. Tuumarsi visited the sick people with bits of food.

In one of the houses an elderly woman lay on the benches, unable to move. She lay there coughing and wheezing. She was so emaciated that her ribs almost poked out of her skin. Tuumarsi asked if she was able to eat. No, was the reply, she can't eat anything, she takes only a bit of water. Her mouth and throat are so dried that she is incapable of forcing down even a little bite. Her old disease now has the upper hand. Death can happen at any time, and that is probably what's best for her.

The next day people heard that she was dead.

On the other side of the benches lay a boy, an orphan, who had been weak since childhood. When he saw Tuumarsi come in with food in his hand, he smiled and reached out to him with a trembling hand. Tuumarsi could not help but think of his own children, and full of sympathy, he gave the boy a piece of dried meat. The boy thanked him with a barely audible voice, and moved the food to his mouth. Then he uttered a cry of pain and spat two teeth out into his hand. Crying, he pushed the food inside his anorak and grabbed his mouth.

Tuumarsi couldn't stand it any more. He left behind some of the food he had brought and hurried out of the house.

He went over to another house. On the corner of the benches sat a woman who had had a baby a while ago. The child did not survive though, as its mother didn't have any milk. The youngest child held onto its mothers limp breasts with its hands and tried to suck something out of the teats. The child was almost completely skin and bones, and clearly didn't have much time left to live. The other children fought over the food Tuumarsi brought. Their father sat with a bowed head on a chest at the window. Tuumarsi asked how he was. A stupid and unnecessary question to ask a man in that situation. But one had to say something.

"The worst of it all is seeing the hungry children and not having anything to give them to eat. The next day they ask for food, but what can I do? In the autumn we thought we had enough winter stores for the entire season, and then some. But it turned out there wasn't even enough for half the winter."

"This is the case for everyone. Normally the winter stores should have been enough. Nobody could have predicted what is happening now," Tuumarsi said.

A whine was heard from the area below the benches. Shortly after, a dog came out. It wasn't that emaciated, compared to the inhabitants of the house.

"Oh, so you still have a dog," Tuumarsi said, bemusedly. "I was under the impression that there were no more dogs left. So you do have a few food stores."

"That was our son's – Ujuaansi's dog. You know, our son was one of those that perished during the hurricane. He got the dog when it was a puppy, and since he cared so much for it, we, his mother and I, have cared for it after his death and taken care of it as if it were a member of the family. We didn't have the heart to put it down. We let it stay here, where it's home is. Now we've agreed to let it live for as long as it can. It won't die of hunger so long as it subsists on scraps of skin. We don't look on it as a food reserve, it isn't even enough for one meal."

When Tuumarsi came home, he sat for a long time without saying anything. His thoughts were occupied by what he had seen.

He could see that his children had lost some of their fat. They didn't get as much to eat as before either. The rationing included them too. But if it continued to go as it did now, if a time came when there wasn't any more food in the house—no, he dared not even think of that possibility; when he felt that the family was suffering hunger, then he would make every effort to acquire food for them at any cost. He took care not to lose weight in an attempt to preserve his strength. He let Iisaaq get a larger ration for the same reason. And it hurt him to see Iisaaq share his food with his siblings, but he didn't have the courage to prevent him from doing so. He himself only ate when the children were not present. The most visibly emaciated was his wife. She lost her appetite when she heard the children begging for food.

They could still allow themselves a low flame in the lamps, but only enough to give them a bit of heat. You would rather have more light and heat, but they also needed blubber for their diet consisting of dried meat and fish, which was all they had to eat.

15.

One morning, Tuumarsi's children had been out. When they came home they told of what they had seen: One of the other children chewing on an old kamik sole. In their childish naivety, they asked their mother whether old kamik soles tasted good.

Kaluliit looked, in shock, at her husband. "No," she said. "You mustn't do anything like that ever. You will only become more hungry doing so."

Tuumarsi was also shocked. Was the need so great that people had begun to do those kinds of things? While the children were away, he went over to the storehouse to see how much was left of the stores, and to his dismay he found that the stocks had shrunk quite considerably. There was no more to spare for the others. That which remained had to be saved for his own household.

When he came back, he said to his wife, "Kaluliit, I have decided not to give any more to the others. I would hate to be considered a miser, but that which remains of the most essential parts of the stocks won't stretch to more than a few days for us alone." His wife did not reply, and he had barely finished speaking before a woman came in. Crying, she asked for a bit of food for her children, who hadn't had anything to eat for two days, and were clearly weakened.

Tuumarsi said nothing. He went out and came back with a handful of ammassat and gave them to the woman.

"This is all we can spare. And this is probably the last time I can give anything away, as we don't have much left."

The woman hid the little fish under her anorak and hurried out. On her way home she took a single one out and put it in her mouth. She too was very hungry.

Deaths became more frequent—it was first and foremost the weak people with illnesses, such as consumption, and infants that went without mother's milk.

One morning a new death was reported: The woman who had begged from Tuumarsi's family two days ago had died along with one of her children. When their house-mates had discovered them, rigor mortis had already set in. These were the first regular deaths from starvation, but more were to come. Tuumarsi didn't want to wait any longer. He wanted to somehow go to get help. He was the hunter with the most strength left, and he was probably also the only one who could carry out such a relief operation. That it might potentially cost him his life, well, that was a risk he had to take.

16.

The day dawned with fine and calm weather. As was his habit, Tuumarsi got up early and went outside. The fine weather with blue sky and a completely white sea felt as if nature was teasing him. The sea should be blue, not white with packed ice, and if it had to be white, it should be white with cresting waves.

The compact ice, however, gave him an idea. It should be possible to walk on it with the kayak on ones head, until reaching the ice-edge. Then one might – if all went well – reach the ice-less sea and head for the location of the colony. It was risky, but what else could he do? He was of no use here, neither for his family nor for the others.

He went into the house and said what he intended to do. His wife burst into tears and forbade him doing so. She preferred that he stay at home so he could be with them during the difficult time, rather than risking his life on the ice-filled sea.

The children had woken in the meantime, and the first words they said were food. And that made Tuumarsi stick even firmer to his decision. They began the day with their usual morning song:

Jesus, to my heart
let your light appear.
Let the glory of the world
never tempt me.
From worldly things, let my thoughts stray away,
and the thought of my death occupy me alone.

Tuumarsi had never closely considered the words in this psalm. But in this moment he felt the words had a message for him. He grew confused. Should they adapt their lives in such a way that they didn't need to worry about worldly things, about the necessary of maintaining life? Should they, in a situation such as this, simply accept their fate? If that was the case there would have been no point in him ever having to leave, in storms or bad weather, to gather food for all of them, and he had done that, even when there was food in the house. Now though, in the worst situation they had ever experienced, he had done nothing to provide the essentials for the preservation of life. He had to do his duty.

Duty and the will of man must conquer all. He made ready to leave. He looked seriously at his son Iisaaq, as if he left the duty of providing to him.

Weeping, his wife and children watched as he wandered over the ice with his kayak on his head. So too did the men, who stood at their usual gathering point. Only when he had vanished behind the icebergs did the family enter their house with a feeling of infinite loneliness.

17.

Finally, at long last, Tuumarsi made it out to the ice edge. Since the sea was calm, he didn't have much trouble getting into his kayak and moved carefully between the ice chunks out towards the open sea. If only a seal would pop up, he thought.

He didn't know exactly where he was. He couldn't get his bearings from the land, as the view to the lowlands was covered by icebergs, and because the fog hid the mountains. The sea was calm, and there was only one thing he worried about. That was the possibility that the fog might condense into snow, which, when the wind picked up, might develop into a snowstorm.

The fog bank drifted down and revealed the tops of the fells. There, towards land, towered the Chest-mountain, easily recognizable by its peculiar shape. His thoughts had until now been occupied by the prey of the sea, but the sight of the Chest-mountain led his thoughts to something else, namely the food items from the shop, which were usually stored in the chest. But, what was one to do with them? They were not as nourishing as the food provided by the sea, and they could only be purchased with money, and nobody had any. The food obtained from the sea was something else. It consisted of meat and blubber, food no Greenlander could go without, and which could be obtained without payment. There was nothing else to do. He was on his way to the colony, it didn't matter if it was near or far, whether they had money or not. There were no other places to go.

Now he thought of his family. Who was to provide for them? Would they have anything to live off? All these heavy thoughts couldn't make him give up his journey.

He scouted for seals so intensely that he sometimes convinced himself that he saw a seal appear, but the moment he reached for his harpoon to throw it, the seal would disappear. He had to smile—knowing the phenomenon of hallucinations all too well.

Where had the Chest-mountain gone? He stared in the direction where the Chest-mountain should have been, but there was nothing to be seen. What he feared had come to pass. The storm was on its way, and at this time of year that could mean only one thing: a snow storm.

What should he do now? He had, through many years of the hunting life and travels at sea, developed his instinct and learned to rely on it. He wrinkled his forehead and looked around to all sides. At the same time he turned and headed for land. It was now all about finding some place where he could get ashore before the storm picked up. It wasn't because he didn't think he'd be able to manage at sea, that wasn't what he was afraid of. He was wearing a full-fur and still had his strength. What he was afraid of was that the storm might move the ice, putting the kayak in a dangerous situation. If only he could reach static ice and make his way up on it with his kayak intact, then he'd have good odds of reaching land and getting to safety. From there he'd be able to wait for the weather to improve.

It didn't take long before the snow storm came in from the north east. It was impossible to row directly towards it, and he had to change his course, so he had the wind at his side. Nothing could be seen. Everything was wreathed in snow. He desperately hoped that the ice wouldn't move too much, otherwise he'd risk the kayak skin tearing, preventing him from getting ashore. He hoped that it wouldn't happen, but on the other hand he knew from experience that it could. He concentrated on paying attention to his surroundings, and he was ready to slow when he moved between the ice pieces.

Suddenly his oar struck something hard and could only be ice. He brushed his eyes with the back of his glove, so as to better look around. Yes, there was ice all around him. He must have entered the outermost ice belt.

18.

The situation was dangerous. It was impossible to get ones bearings, and he didn't know how far it was to the more solid ice.

Tuumarsi rowed forwards carefully. He hit ice with almost every oar stroke, and on several occasions he felt his kayak lift up, yet he managed. He felt that he wasn't far from the ice edge, as the pieces were so close to each other.

The next problem would be how to make it to the ice edge, or to the more solid part of the ice, where he would be able to get out of the kayak. The last solution entailed a great risk. If he managed to get on an ice floe, then he risked it drifting out, or that another ice floe turn up and topple the one he was on, as turbulent as the sea was. In the best case he could try to reach shore by leaping from ice floe to ice floe with his kayak, but that could be deadly dangerous.

These speculations were quickly brought to an end. Tuumarsi felt his legs were wet. The kayak was already lying very low, and the water soon reached his waist.

In the moment the ice pieces laid themselves over the kayak, he placed his kayak oar across it, and tried to get out in one movement. He experienced a shortness of breath and realized that he was under water. He held his breath and grabbed a hold of the cross-strap in front of him and once again tried to get out, and this time he managed. When he again managed to get his head above water he took a couple of deep breaths and then held his breath again. When he once more popped out of the water, he stretched out his arms and got a hold of an ice floe, and after repeated efforts he managed to get up and lie on his stomach across it. Then he filled his lungs with more proper breaths.

He saved himself. The kayak though, the one he was to use as a rescue craft wandering across the ice floes, had vanished into the sea. The equally invaluable kayak oar had also vanished.

Having rested for a while, he sniffed the wind and got up. Then he took the first steps towards land. The outwards drift of the ice could be fatal for him. He was wet from top to toe, and if he didn't move fast, then he'd risk freezing stuck.

She set off on his way. On transitioning from one ice floe to the next, he would often fall in the water. Where the ice pieces lay too far from each other he would have to wait until they collided and created a crossing. When he reached a larger ice floe, he beat his arms against his body to gain some heat. His trousers and kamiks were frozen stiff, but in spite of this he was in good spirits. He was sure he would reach the static ice, as the ice pieces lay closer together now. He knew that there was no help to be found on the land he currently angled towards. The belief in God's help and compassion however, kept his spirits up.

From the positions of the ice pieces, he reckoned that he was approaching the coast. He had thus avoided death at sea, but what then? The land would not give him options for survival.

Still he wouldn't give up. He could dig himself down into the snow. When the weather improved and the sun shone, he might be able to dry his clothes, somewhat, and there had to be birds on the land as well as the beach, which he might down with thrown rocks. There were also always some types of seaweed and mussels to be found on the beach. But the land he reached could not be anything other than an island, and without a kayak he wouldn't be able to leave it.

When he reached the static ice, he stood there and looked towards the sea. There was nothing to see. Everything was wreathed in snow. Only the booming of the ice pieces colliding could be heard, accompanied by the whooshing of the storm.

He wandered onwards and reached the beach. Discouraged, he went up onto land and sought out a place where he could find shelter. In the desperate situation that he was now in, he couldn't keep back tears, and occasionally would wipe his eyes with his sleeve. Suddenly it grew calm around him, and he realized that he had reached shelter. Muttering to himself, he dug at the snow in front of a slope and crawled in and covered himself. A moment later he lost consciousness.

19.

Tuumarsi didn't know how long he lain unconscious. When he awoke, he poked his head out of the snow and looked around in an attempt to gain his bearings. Everything he had been through he perceived to be a dream, and in truth it wasn't the first time he had dreamed such things. He convinced himself that he had woken up at home in his house, and that he was looking out the window, while from time to time looking at the sleeping children. Eventually he realized this wasn't a dream.

Everything that had happened, his battle against the elements, his rescue, and how he had dug himself down into the snow, was real.

He felt remarkable calm. He covered himself with snow again, and his thoughts were now fully occupied with his family. Were they waiting for him to come home? There was probably not much food left, but there was the possibility that the northern storm had pushed the ice out so the hunters could hunt. Thankfully there were others that could take care of the family if he didn't come home. And if God could provide food for the ravens, then he could provide food for those left behind. He tried to sing a psalm that he happened to think of, but he was too weak to sing. He prayed for God to take care of his family and left their fate in His hands. He did not pray for help for himself, but simply for God's presence.

He realized evening had come. He investigated the place where he had found rest. Perhaps he could find a better one. Then he realized that he was in a hollow beneath a slope. He made himself comfortable as best he could and once again covered himself with snow. Only his face was free.

The moon appeared from behind the clouds and shone on the area around him. The snow storm had stopped, and only the drifting snow danced across the earth. Many types of stories that he heard over time cropped up in his memory. It was as if they were being recounted by the moon. He felt as if he was listening to the monotonous, soporific voice of a storyteller. And it wasn't long, either, before he fell asleep.

How remarkable! Where was he now? On a plain not far from the beach stood a group of people. He himself lay in a hollow under a slope and watched them. They were men he knew, all the men that had perished in their kayaks, including his own son along with the others that had perished in the storm a couple years ago. Some had full-furs on and had their kayak-oars in their hands. Others wore half-furs and yet more wore anoraks. He could hear waves beating against the beach. Yes, even the boom of a hollow under the fast ice could be clearly heard. From time to time he heard the cackle of a grouse from the fell behind him.

While he regarded all this and listened to the sounds, he heard one of the men say: "Do you hear the cackling of the grouse? When it is heard at night, then it can only mean one thing . . . let us do for him as we usually do for others."

Tuumarsi was about to ask what all this meant when the men struck up a psalm that he had never heard before.

Judging by the words, he thought he could understand that the psalm was about death. Was it him they sang for? But he was healthy and hearty and had nothing wrong with him.

When the psalm finished, the vision slowly blurred and finally vanished completely. But he could still hear the melody of the psalm, and he could also remember the words. Then he heard the rushing of the wind—he must have regained consciousness—but he wasn't aware of where he was. All he could feel was lying nice and warm beneath the blanket. Then the memories arrived in a flurry, and shortly after, the image of the men that had sung for him. And he recognized several of the men–though they all had perished in kayaks. Then the image changed, he saw himself in a kayak on the troubled seas. He also remembered his departure from home, but how his journey ended, that he could not recall.

20.

He must have lost consciousness for a while. When he came to, he thought of God's vicissitudes. God had granted him skill, strength and endurance, everything he had needed in his profession. Had he, Tuumarsi, thanked God enough for that? He was now aware that the psalm he heard was the psalm of his death. And now, in the last phase of his life, what was he to say to God in thanks for his kindnesses to him? He was sure that God would receive him well and give him glory's unwithering wreath. And with that conviction he now found life on earth tiresome and futile. He had, until now, been happy with the life God had given him, but now, at the end of his earthly life, he found it endlessly empty and unimportant. "I am on my way to God, and God will greet me. He has created us to live off the sea, and it is our duty to adapt ourselves to that. Now my life's work is done, and I go to my maker in peace."

Once again he heard the notes of the psalm, and it dawned on Tuumarsi that he could remember the words:

Death, take me away, for I am tired,
bring me up to the halls of heaven.
Blissful is he who is blessed,
who deserves the unwithering wreath.

That was all he wanted to say. With this psalm verse he gave expression to everything he felt.

Suddenly his mother stood in front of him. She took him by the hand and placed them, his and hers, on his chest. As he closed his eyes, his heart beat for the last time.

The moon appeared from behind the clouds and delivered its rays to his resting place.